# PLATO'S TIMAEUS

**The Library of Liberal Arts**
OSKAR PIEST, FOUNDER

The Library of Liberal Arts

# PLATO'S TIMAEUS

Translated by
FRANCIS M. CORNFORD
*Late Laurence Professor of Ancient Philosophy and Fellow of*
*Trinity College in the University of Cambridge*
and reprinted from his work, *Plato's Cosmology*

Edited by OSKAR PIEST

• • • • • • • • • • • • • • • • • • • • • • • • • • • • • • • • • • • • • • •

The Library of Liberal Arts
*published by*

THE **BOBBS-MERRILL** COMPANY, INC.
A SUBSIDIARY OF HOWARD W. SAMS & CO., INC.
*Publishers* • INDIANAPOLIS • NEW YORK

COPYRIGHT ©, 1959
THE LIBERAL ARTS PRESS, INC.
All Rights Reserved
Printed in the United States of America
Library of Congress Catalog Card Number: 59-11680
Second Printing

# EDITOR'S PREFACE

This edition presents Francis M. Cornford's translation of *Plato's Timaeus* which has been reprinted from his standard work, *Plato's Cosmology. The Timaeus of Plato translated with a running commentary.*

The editor gratefully acknowledges the approval of the original publishers, Routledge and Kegan Paul, Ltd., London, for this special edition, and also their permission to include from Cornford's commentary a number of explanatory notes which seem to be indispensable for an understanding of the argument.

The separate edition of the *Timaeus* has been designed for a less detailed study of the Dialogue than *Plato's Cosmology* affords, and is offered for this limited purpose only. It is not meant to be a substitute for *Plato's Cosmology*, which is also available in this series.

The text of the Dialogue is a faithful reproduction of Cornford's text. Regarding the notes the editor has taken some liberties—either taken notes from the text and incorporated them in the footnotes or abridged footnotes, usually omitting textual criticism.

O.P.

# CONTENTS

LIST OF ABBREVIATIONS .............................. viii
PREFACE ........................................... ix
INTRODUCTION ...................................... xvii

## THE TIMAEUS

| 17a-27b | INTRODUCTORY CONVERSATION ............ | 3 |

### THE DISCOURSE OF TIMAEUS

| 27c-29d | PRELUDE ............................. | 15 |
| 29d-47e | I. THE WORKS OF REASON ............... | 19 |
| | The Body of the World (31b-34a) 21 | |
| | The World-Soul (34a-40d) ....... 23 | |
| | Table of Celestial motions ...... 33 | |
| | The Human Soul and Body (40d-47e) ....................... 35 | |
| 47e-69a | II. WHAT COMES ABOUT OF NECESSITY ...... | 45 |
| 69a-92c | III. THE CO-OPERATION OF REASON AND NECESSITY ................................. | 81 |

# LIST OF ABBREVIATIONS

| | |
|---|---|
| A.-H. | = Archer-Hind, R. D. The Timaeus of Plato, London, 1888. |
| Albinus | = Ἀλκινόου (sic) διδασκαλικὸς τῶν Πλάτωνος δογμάτων, ed. Hermann, Platonis Dialogi, Lipsiae, 1892, vi, pp. 152 ff. |
| Apelt | = Platon's Dialoge Timaios und Kritias übersetzt und erläutert von O. Apelt, Leipzig, 1922. |
| Chalcidius | = Platonis Timaeus interprete Chalcidio cum eiusdem commentario, ed. J. Wrobel, Lipsiae, MDCCCLXXVI. |
| Fraccaroli | = Il Timeo trad. da Giuseppe Fraccaroli, Torino, 1906. |
| Pr. | = Procli Diodochi in Platonis Timaeum commentaria, ed. E. Diehl, Lipsiae, MCMVI. |
| Rivaud | = Platon, Tome x, Timée, Critias, texte établi et traduit par Albert Rivaud, Paris, 1925. |
| Theon | = Theon of Smyrna, τῶν κατὰ τὸ μαθηματικὸν χρησίμων εἰς τὴν Πλάτωνος ἀνάγνωσιν, ed. Dupuis, Paris, 1892. |
| Tr. | = Taylor, A. E., A Commentary on Plato's Timaeus, Oxford, 1928. |

# TRANSLATOR'S PREFACE*

This book is constructed on the same plan as an earlier volume in the series, *Plato's Theory of Knowledge*. It contains a translation of the *Timaeus* interspersed with a commentary discussing each problem of interpretation—and there are many hitherto unsolved—as it arises. My first aim has been to render Plato's words as closely as I can. Anyone who attempts to reproduce his exalted poetical style must face the certainty of failure, with the added risk of falsifying the sense, especially by misleading reminiscences of the English Bible. The commentary is designed to guide the reader through a long and intricate argument and to explain what must remain obscure in the most faithful translation; for the *Timaeus* covers an immense field at the cost of compressing the thought into the smallest space. Only with some such aid can students of theology and philosophy have access to a document which has deeply influenced mediaeval and modern speculation. I have tried not to confuse the interpretation of the text with the construction of theories of wider scope. The later Platonism is a subject on which agreement may never be reached; but there is some hope of persuading scholars that a Greek sentence means one thing rather than another.

The translation follows Burnet's text, except where I have given reasons for departing from it or proposed corrections of passages that are probably or certainly corrupt. For the interpretation I have consulted, in the first instance, the commentaries of Proclus and Chalcidius, the fragment of Galen's commentary lately re-edited by Schröder, the relevant treatises of Plutarch, and Theon of Smyrna, who preserves valuable extracts from Dercylides and Adrastus. The careful summary of the *Timaeus* in the *Didascalicus* of the Middle Platonist Albinus deserves more attention than it receives. Among the

* [Reprinted in its entirety from Cornford: *Plato's Cosmology* (LLA 101)—Ed.]

moderns I have drawn freely upon Martin's admirable *Études sur le Timée de Platon,* Archer-Hind's commentary, and the translations of Apelt, Fraccaroli, Rivaud, and Professor A. E. Taylor.[1]

More useful than any of these has been Professor Taylor's *Commentary*. His wide learning and untiring industry have amassed a great quantity of illustrative material, and he has cleared up the meaning of many sentences hitherto misunderstood. These amendments will pass into the common stock of future editors and translators, and I have for the most part adopted them tacitly. It is unfortunate that I should so often have had to quote his views where it was necessary to give reasons for dissent. My notes, accordingly, do not indicate the extent of a debt which I here acknowledge with gratitude.

On many of the larger questions of interpretation, however, I differ widely from Professor Taylor. He has launched in this volume a new Taylorian heresy. After confounding the persons of Socrates and Plato in earlier books, he has now divided the substance of Plato and Timaeus. All the ancient Platonists from Aristotle to Simplicius and all mediaeval and modern scholars to our own day have assumed that this dialogue contains the mature doctrine of its author. Professor Taylor holds that they have been mistaken. He writes:

> It is in fact the main thesis of the present interpretation that the teaching of Timaeus can be shown to be in detail exactly what we should expect in a fifth-century Italian Pythagorean who was also a medical man, that it is, in fact, a deliberate attempt to amalgamate Pythagorean religion and mathematics with Empedoclean biology, and thus correctly represents the same tendency in fifth-century thought for which the name, e.g. of Philolaus stands in the history of philosophy. If this view is sound, it follows that it is a mistake to look in the *Timaeus* for any revelation of the distinctively Platonic doctrines, the ἴδια Πλάτωνος as Aristotle calls them (*Met.* A. 987a, 31), by which Platonism is discriminated from Pythagoreanism, or for a "later Platonic theory" which can be set in opposition to the type of doc-

[1] I regret that I did not learn that Mr. R. G. Bury's translation had appeared until it was too late to make use of it.

trine expounded in the *Phaedo*. I shall set myself in commenting on the relevant passages to argue in detail that we do not, in fact, find any of the doctrines Aristotle thought distinctive of Plato taught in the *Timaeus* or in any other dialogue. But, on the other hand, what the *Timaeus* loses, if my view is a sound one, as an exposition of Platonism it gains as a source of light on fifth-century Pythagoreanism. If I am interpreting it on right lines, it is incomparably the most important document we possess for the history of early Greek scientific thought.

Further on, Professor Taylor describes Plato's plan in more detail. "The formula for the physics and physiology of the dialogue is that it is an attempt to graft Empedoclean biology on the stock of Pythagorean mathematics" (p. 18). This fusion, he adds, could not be completely carried out. There were incongruities which lead Timaeus "into a variety of real inconsistencies which culminate in an absolutely unqualified contradiction between a medical or physiological 'determinism' (*Tim.* 86b-87b) and a religious and ethical doctrine of human 'freedom,'" which is undoubtedly Pythagorean.

Plato repeatedly warns us in this very dialogue that cosmology and physical science in general can never be more than "provisional." It is at best made up of tales "like the truth." Hence Plato was not likely to feel himself responsible for the details of any of his speaker's theories. All that is required by his own principles is that they shall be more or less "like" the truth, i.e. that they shall be the best approximations to it which could be expected from a geometer-biologist of the fifth century. In other words, we are entitled to say that Plato thought the view which arose from the fusion of Pythagoras with Empedocles the most promising line in fifth-century science and the one most directly connected with his own developments. It does not follow that *any* theory propounded by Timaeus would have been accepted by Plato as it stands. The way in which Timaeus is made at each chief new step in his narrative to insist on the highly provisional character of his speculations is a most significant feature of the dialogue, to which no one as yet seems to have done full justice. What Plato himself really thought about a good deal of Empedocles has to be learned not from our dialogue but from *Laws* x, where

Empedocles more than anyone else is plainly aimed at in the exposure of the defects of "naturalism" (pp. 18-19).

According to this theory, then, Plato, having occasion to give an account of the nature of the visible world, concocted an amalgam of two philosophies belonging to the previous century, although he knew them to be incompatible and largely disapproved of one of them. All he wanted was something "like the truth." What he actually produced was not a picture that he himself could accept as more like the truth than any other, but the best that could be expected from an imaginary eclectic, of two or three generations earlier, attempting to combine irreconcilables.

I cannot think that this theory will be accepted. The improbability is so great that overwhelming proof must be required. The evidence, if it existed, could hardly have been overlooked by all those ancient authorities whose knowledge of Platonism and its antecedents was far greater than any we can ever hope to possess. Professor Taylor rightly insists that the student should know what the men who had heard Plato's doctrines from his own lips or from his immediate disciples supposed him to mean; and how he was understood by men of real learning like Posidonius, Plutarch, and Atticus, and even later by men versed in the earlier literature like Plotinus and Proclus. The chief value of his own commentary lies in the exhaustive summaries of these ancient opinions. But if his theory is sound, how is it that not one of them furnishes a single unambiguous statement to the effect that the doctrines of the *Timaeus* are not Plato's own? Aristotle was living and working with Plato when the dialogue was written. Why does he never use the *Timaeus* as "a source of light on fifth-century Pythagoreanism" or refer to it as "a document for the history of early Greek scientific thought," a subject in which he was much interested? How is it that Theophrastus (as Professor Taylor remarks, p. 1) "treats the whole account of the sensible qualities given in our dialogue as the views of Plato," without a hint that they are really no more than the best that could be expected from a geometer-biologist of the previous century?

From all that we know of Theophrastus' History of Physical Opinions it is clear that he used the *Timaeus* as his main source of Plato's physical doctrine. Aristotle and Theophrastus must have known the true character of the work. Both wrote at length on the history of philosophy. Neither left on record so much as a suspicion that Plato was really fabricating a medley of obsolete theories for which he acknowledged no responsibility. Had such a suspicion been expressed in any of their works now lost to us, it could not have escaped the notice of the later ancient commentators, who studied the *Timaeus* line by line and sought for light upon its meaning in every available quarter. The discovery would then have robbed the dialogue of all authority. Not only would it have lost its value as an expression of Plato's mind, but to the ancients it would have been useless as a record of fifth-century speculation. Possessing the original documents on which it was based, they would have contemplated with more amazement than interest the ingenuity spent in conjuring out of them an incoherent system which nobody had ever held.

It is hard to understand how anyone acquainted with the literature and art of the classical period can imagine that the greatest philosopher of that period, at the height of his powers, could have wasted his time on so frivolous and futile an exercise in pastiche. What could have been his motive? Nowhere, in all his seven hundred pages, has Professor Taylor really faced this question; yet it surely calls for an answer. When an archaeologist unearths a temple in a sixth-century style of architecture, it never occurs to him to doubt whether the sculpture may not be the work of Praxiteles or Scopas, deliberately faking an archaic manner. He knows that such things were not done till the blaze of creative genius had died down; the foundations of Wardour Street were laid in Alexandria. Yet such a supposition would be every whit as probable as Professor Taylor's thesis.

The reader who does not accept that thesis will find himself somewhat bewildered by attempts to prove that Timaeus says one thing while Plato believes another. There are two other tendencies, running through the whole commentary, which seem to me to distort the picture. One is the suggestion that Plato (or Timaeus?) is at heart a monotheist and not far from being a Christian.[2] The Demiurge is not fully recognized as a mythical figure, but credited with attributes belonging to the Creator of Genesis or even to the God of the New Testament. Another is the practice of translating Plato's words into the terms of Professor Whitehead's philosophy. That philosophy could not have existed before the Theory of Relativity; and its author, having very unfamiliar ideas to express, uses common words in senses so peculiar and esoteric that no one can follow him without a glossary. Consider the following definitions of an "occasion" and an "event":

> Each monadic creature is a mode of the process of "feeling" the world, of housing the world in one unit of complex feeling, in every way determinate. Such a unit is an "actual occasion"; it is the ultimate creature derivative from the creative process. The term "event" is used in a more general sense. An event is a nexus of actual occasions inter-related in some determinate fashion in some extensive quantum: it is either a nexus in its formal completeness, or it is an objectified nexus. One actual occasion is a limiting type of event. The most general sense of the meaning of change is "the differences between actual occasions in one event." For example, a molecule is a historic route of actual occasions; and such a route is an "event." Now the motion of the molecule is nothing else than the differences between the successive occasions of its life-history in respect to the extensive quanta from which they arise; and the changes in the molecule are the consequential differences in the actual occasions (*Process and Reality,* pp. 111-12).

It is true that Professor Whitehead has been profoundly influenced by Jowett's translation, and that his eternal objects have a definite affinity to Plato's eternal Forms. But there is more of Plato in the *Adventures of Ideas* than there is of Whitehead in the *Timaeus.* The modern reader is likely to be misled by the constant use of Whitehead's "event" as equivalent to Plato's γιγνόμενον. Moreover, Plato expressly declares

[2] Examples will be found in the notes on 29d-30c and 69c, 3.

that his Forms "never enter into anything else anywhere" (52a) —a cardinal point of difference between himself and Aristotle. Yet Professor Taylor writes: "γένεσις . . . is, in fact, the 'ingredience of objects into events,' by which the 'passage' of nature is constituted. . . . The famous Forms . . . are what Whitehead calls 'objects,' and the point of insistence upon their reality is that Nature is not made up of the mere succession of events, that the passage of nature is a process of 'ingredience' of objects into events" (p. 131). According to Professor Taylor's main thesis, the philosophy of our dialogue belongs to a period which already seemed archaic to Aristotle: he regularly speaks of the fifth-century thinkers as "the primitives" (οἱ ἀρχαῖοι). Even if we restore this philosophy to Plato, it cannot usefully be paraphrased in terms which have first acquired their technical meaning in our own life-time. It is puzzling to find the contents of Timaeus' discourse represented at one moment as more antique than Plato and at the next as more modern (and considerably more Christian) than Herbert Spencer. Accordingly, while every student must acknowledge a great debt to Professor Taylor's researches, there is still room for a commentary based on the traditional assumptions and attempting to illustrate Plato's thought in the historical setting of Plato's century.

Friends and colleagues have generously helped me with their advice on matters in which I needed a judgment more competent than my own. Sir Thomas Heath, whose masterly works on Greek mathematics I have constantly consulted and never in vain, has written long and careful answers to my inquiries. Professor Onians has allowed me to use freely the proofs of his valuable book, *The Origins of Greek and Roman Thought*. I am also specially indebted to Dr. W. H. S. Jones, Professor D. S. Robertson, Mr. R. P. Winnington-Ingram, and Mr. R. Hackforth.

F. M. C.

CAMBRIDGE
1937

# INTRODUCTION*

The *Timaeus* belongs to the latest group of Plato's works: *Sophist* and *Statesman*, *Timaeus* and *Critias*, *Philebus*, *Laws*. The whole group must fall within the last twenty years of his life, which ended in 347 B.C. at the age of eighty or eighty-one. The *Laws* is the only dialogue that is certainly later than the *Timaeus* and *Critias*. It is probable, then, that Plato was nearer seventy than sixty when he projected the trilogy, *Timaeus, Critias, Hermocrates*—the most ambitious design he had ever conceived. Too ambitious, it would seem; for he abandoned it when he was less than halfway through. The *Critias* breaks off in an unfinished sentence; the *Hermocrates* was never written. Only the *Timaeus* is complete; but its introductory part affords some ground for a conjectural reconstruction of the whole plan.

The conversation in this dialogue and its sequel is supposed to take place at Athens on the day of the Panathenaea. We are to imagine that, on the previous day, Socrates has been discoursing to Critias, his two guests from Italy and Sicily, Timaeus of Locri and Hermocrates of Syracuse, and a fourth unnamed person who is today absent through indisposition. The Panathenaic festival would provide an obvious occasion for the strangers' presence in Athens, as it does for the visit of Parmenides and Zeno in another of the late dialogues.[1]

The Athenian Critias is an old man, who finds it easier to remember the long-distant past than what happened yesterday, and speaks of his boyhood as "very long ago," when the poems of Solon could be described as a novelty. He cannot, therefore,

* [Reprinted in its entirety from Cornford: *Plato's Cosmology* (LLA 101)—Ed.]

[1] *Parm.* 127d. The comparison is made by Pr. i, 84. That "the festival of the goddess" (Athena) mentioned at 21a and 26e is the Panathenaea is clear from the context in both places and would never have been doubted but for the unfounded notion that Socrates is supposed to have narrated on the previous day the whole of the *Republic*, or a substantial part of it, as it stands in our texts. This will be considered below.

be the Critias who was Plato's mother's cousin and one of the Thirty Tyrants. He must be the grandfather of that Critias and Plato's great-grandfather.[2] He tells us that he was eighty years younger than his own grandfather, the Critias who was Solon's friend.

Hermocrates, according to Proclus (on 20a) and modern scholars, is the Syracusan who defeated the Athenian expedition to Sicily in Plato's childhood (415-413 B.C.). Thucydides (vi, 72) describes him as a man of outstanding intelligence, conspicuous bravery, and great military experience. At his first appearance in the History (iv, 58) he delivers a wise speech at a conference of Sicilian states, advising them to make peace among themselves and warning them of the danger of Athenian aggression. Evidently at that date (424 B.C.) he was already a prominent figure in Sicilian politics. After the defeat of the Athenian expedition he was banished by the democratic party. He lost his life in an attempt to reinstate himself by force, probably in 407 B.C. In the present gathering of philosophers and statesmen he is pre-eminently the man of action. Since the dialogue that was to bear his name was never written, we can only guess why Plato chose him. It is curious to reflect that, while Critias is to recount how the prehistoric Athens of nine thousand years ago had repelled the invasion from Atlantis and saved the Mediterranean peoples from slavery, Hermocrates would be remembered by the Athenians as the man who had repulsed their own greatest effort at imperialist expansion. He had also attempted to reform from within his native city, Syracuse, the scene of Plato's own abortive essays toward the reconstruction of existing society.

There is no evidence for the historic existence of Timaeus of Locri. If he did exist, we know nothing whatever about him beyond Socrates' description of him as a man well-born and rich, who had held the highest offices at Locri and become eminent in philosophy (20a), and Critias' remark that

[2] See Burnet, *Gk. Phil.* i, 338, and Appendix. Tr., p. 23. Diehl, P.-W., *Real-Encycl.*, s.v. Kritias.

Timaeus was the best astronomer in the party and had made a special study of the nature of the universe. This is consistent with his being a man in middle life, contemporary with Hermocrates.[3] The very fact that a man of such distinction has left not the faintest trace in political or philosophic history is against his claim to be a real person. The probability is that Plato invented him because he required a philosopher of the Western school, eminent both in science and statesmanship, and there was no one to fill the part at the imaginary time of the dialogue. Archytas was of the type required,[4] a brilliant mathematician and seven times *strategus* at Tarentum; but he lived too late: Plato first met him about 388 B.C. In the first century A.D. a treatise *On the Soul of the World and Nature* was forged in the name of Timaeus of Locri. It was taken by the Neoplatonists for a genuine document, whereas it is now seen to be a mere summary of the *Timaeus*. In our dialogue, as Wilamowitz observes (*Platon* i, 591), Timaeus speaks dogmatically, but without any appeal to authority, and we may regard his doctrine simply as Plato's own. So in the *Sophist* Plato speaks through the mouth of an Eleatic, who is yet not a champion of Parmenides' system, but holds a theory of Forms unquestionably Platonic. Plato nowhere says that Timaeus is a Pythagorean. He sometimes fol-

---

[3] I cannot follow Tr.'s inference from Socrates' words that "we cannot imagine him (Timaeus) to be less than seventy and he may be decidedly older" (p. 17). Sir Arthur Eddington and Professor Dirac were both elected into chairs of mathematics at Cambridge in or about their thirtieth years. In the fifth century B.C. a man of that age might easily have read everything written in Greek on physics and mathematics. Nor did the Greeks wait till a man was nearing seventy before electing him to the highest offices. Tr. also says (p. 49) that "the youth of Hermocrates explains why he remains silent throughout the dialogue. Proclus saw that his silence is significant, but did not interpret it correctly." But Hermocrates does make a not unimportant contribution to the conversation on the only occasion offered him (20c), a fact on which Pr. comments. He also speaks in the introductory conversation of the *Critias* (108b) in terms which, with other passages, make it clear that he was to take the leading part in the third dialogue of the trilogy.

[4] As Frank observes, *Plato und d. sog. Pythagoreer*, 129.

lows Empedocles, sometimes Parmenides; indeed he borrows something from every pre-Socratic philosopher of importance, not to mention Plato's contemporaries. Much of the doctrine is no doubt Pythagorean; and this gave the satirist Timon a handle for his spiteful accusation of plagiarism against Plato. When the treatise ascribed to Timaeus had been forged, it was assumed that this was the book from which Plato had copied (Pr. i, 1 and 7).[5] As a consequence, all the doctrines which the forger had found in the *Timaeus* itself were supposed to be of Pythagorean origin. The testimony of later commentators is vitiated by this false assumption.

There is no ground for any conjecture as to the identity of the fourth person, who is absent. The only sensible remark recorded by Proclus is the observation of Atticus that he is presumably another visitor from Italy or Sicily, since Socrates asks Timaeus for news of him (Pr. i, 20). Plato may have wished to keep open the possibility of extending his trilogy to a fourth dialogue and held this unnamed person in reserve.[6] Socrates proposes that the three who are present (not Timaeus alone) shall undertake the whole task which the four were to have shared. He first recapitulates his own discourse of the previous day. Socrates, we are told, had been describing the institutions of a city on the lines of the *Republic*. He had ended by expressing his wish to see this city transferred from the plane of theory to temporal fact. He now gives a summary of his own discourse, in response to Timaeus' request to be reminded of the task to be performed by himself and his friends. Later (20c) it appears that such a reminder was really unnecessary, since the three have talked over the task required of them and have come prepared with a plan for its fulfilment. The summary is, in fact, entirely for the sake of informing the reader of Plato's design to identify the citizens of the ideal state with the prehistoric Athenians of Critias' romance.

From ancient times to the present day many false inferences and theories have been founded on the situation imagined by

[5] For the history of this document, see Tr., p. 39.
[6] So Ritter, *N. Unt.*, 181.

Plato, in spite of his own clear indication conveyed in the statement that the summary actually given is complete: nothing of importance has been omitted (19a,b). Plato could not have stated more plainly that Socrates is not to be supposed to have narrated the whole conversation in the *Republic* as we have it. It follows at once that he did not intend the *Republic* to stand as the first dialogue in his new series.[7] If he had, no recapitulation would have been needed; the stage should have been set in an introduction to the *Republic* itself. But some scholars have seen evidence here for an original edition of the *Republic*, containing only the parts summarized. Such speculations are baseless. The summary is confined to the external institutions of the state outlined in *Republic* ii, 369-v, 471. It is impossible to imagine an edition of the dialogue omitting the whole of the analogy between the structure of the soul and that of the state, the analysis of the individual soul into three parts, and the discussion of the virtues of the individual and of the state; nor could the omission of these topics in the summary be called a matter of no importance. The simple and natural conclusion was drawn long ago by Hirzel.[8] No doubt Plato was thinking of the contents of that part of the *Republic* and intending his readers to recall them; but he was not the slave of his own fictions. There was nothing to prevent him from imagining Socrates describing his ideal state on more than one occasion. He tells us here that Socrates has outlined its institutions, and nothing more, on the previous day. That day, moreover, was not the day after the feast of Bendis (Thargelion 19 or 20), when the conversation with Glaucon and Adeimantus at the house of Cephalus took place, though nothing would have been easier than to mention that date if Plato had meant to identify Socrates' discourse with the narration of the *Republic*. The present

[7] As Pr., for example, imagined (i, 8). In consequence, he and other critics were puzzled how to explain why the *Republic* was to precede the *Timaeus*, and not follow it, as it obviously should (i, 200 ff.).

[8] *Der Dialog.* (1895), i, 257. So Ritter, *N. Unt.* 177, and Friedländer, *Plat. Schr.* 600. Cf. also Rivaud, *Timée*, p. 19.

occasion is "the festival of Athena,"[9] and one to which the projected discourse of Critias is appropriate. As Proclus remarks (i, 172), the Panathenaic discourses regularly celebrated the Athenian victories by land and sea in the Persian Wars, while Critias celebrates Athens by recounting her victory over the invaders from Atlantis. Proclus himself had no doubt that the Lesser Panathenaea was meant; he knew no more than that this festival "came after" the Bendidea and thought it took place "about the same time" (i, 84-5), whereas he knew that the Greater Panathenaea fell in Hecatombaeon (i, 26). Neither festival, in fact, came within two months of the Bendidea. Plato probably intended the Greater Panathenaea. There is no other indication of the dramatic date; and it is unlikely that Plato had troubled himself about the question whether there was any such occasion on which Hermocrates could have visited Athens. The date is of no importance. In his earliest dialogues Plato was concerned to give the Athenians a true impression of Socrates' character and activity, and he was at great pains to recreate the atmosphere of the times. That interest was long past. In the latest group there was no motive to keep up the illusion that the conversations had really taken place. From all this it follows that the dramatic date and setting of the *Republic* have no bearing whatever on the dramatic date of the *Timaeus* trilogy. Also no ground remains for any inference that Plato meant the contents of the later books of the *Republic* to be superseded or corrected by the *Timaeus*.

The design of the present trilogy is thus completely independent of the *Republic*. What was that design? The political question answered in the *Republic* had been: What is the least change in existing society necessary to cure the evils afflicting mankind? Plato had imagined a reformed Greek city-state with institutions based, as he claimed, on the unalterable characteristics of human nature. It appeared to be

[9] 21a, ἐν τῇ πανηγύρει (the word implies an important festival); 26e, τῇ παρούσῃ τῆς θεοῦ θυσίᾳ. There was no such festival on Thargelion 21. The Plynteria came five days later.

just within the bounds of possible realization. Referring to hopes founded on Dion or on the younger Dionysius, he had said that his state might see the light of day, if some prince could be found endowed with the philosophic nature, and if that nature could escape corruption. But toward the end of the *Republic* Plato seems less hopeful, and the state recedes as a pattern laid up in heaven, by which the merits and defects of all existing constitutions might be measured and appraised. Moreover, since that dialogue was written, Plato's Sicilian adventures had ended in disappointment. Accordingly, the discourse recapitulated at the opening of the *Timaeus* covers only the outline of the state given in the earlier books of the *Republic,* ignoring all the later books, which had started from the question how it might be realized in the future and sketched its possible decline through lower forms of polity. The new trilogy is to transfer this state to the plane of actual existence, not in the future, but in the remote past, as the Athens of nine thousand years ago. This is the subject of the *Critias,* introduced at once as the central theme of the whole.

By way of preface, *Timaeus* is to recount his myth of creation, ending with the birth of mankind. The whole movement starts from the ideal world of the Demiurge and the eternal Forms, descending thence to the frame of the visible universe and the nature of man, whose further fortunes Critias will "take over" for his story. Looking deeper, we see that the chief purpose of the cosmological introduction is to link the morality externalized in the ideal society to the whole organization of the world.[10] The *Republic* had dwelt on the structural analogy between the state and the individual soul. Now Plato intends to base his conception of human life, both for the individual and for society, on the inexpugnable foundation of the order of the universe. The parallel of macrocosm and microcosm runs through the whole discourse. True morality is not a product of human evolution, still less the arbitrary enactment of human wills. It is an order and harmony of the soul; and the soul itself is a counterpart, in miniature, of

[10] Cf. Fraccaroli, p. 13.

the soul of the world, which has an everlasting order and harmony of its own, instituted by reason. This order was revealed to every soul before its birth (41e); and it is revealed now in the visible architecture of the heavens. That human morality is so based on the cosmic order had been implied, here or there, in earlier works; but the *Timaeus* will add something more like a demonstration, although in mythical form.

In the next dialogue Critias will repeat the legend learnt by Solon from an Egyptian priest: how primitive Athens (now to be identified with Socrates' ideal state) had defeated the invaders from Atlantis. In the very hour when freedom and civilization were saved for the mediterranean world, the victorious Athenians had themselves been overwhelmed by flood and earthquake. Atlantis also sank beneath the sea and vanished. What was to follow? The story was not to end with the cataclysm of the *Critias;* and the Egyptian priest, discoursing at some length to Solon on these periodic catastrophes in which all but a small remnant of mankind perishes, has explained how the seeds of a new civilization are preserved either on the mountains or in the river valleys, according as the destruction is by flood or fire. When it is by flood, as at the end of Critias' story, the cities on the plains are overwhelmed; only the mountain shepherds survive, and all culture is lost. Taking up the story at this point, what could Hermocrates do, if not describe the re-emergence of culture in the Greece of prehistoric and historic times? If so, the projected contents of the unwritten dialogue are to be found in the third and subsequent books of the *Laws*. There, after some preliminary ramblings about music and wine in Books i and ii, the Athenian settles down to business at the opening of Book iii with the question: What is the origin of society and government? In the immensity of past time myriads of states have arisen and perished, reproducing again and again the same types of constitution. How do they arise? Mankind has often been almost destroyed by flood, plagues, and many other causes; only a small remnant is left. Imagine one such destruction—the Deluge. The herdsmen on the mountain-tops alone survived, while the cities on the plains or near the sea were overwhelmed. All arts and inventions perished; all statecraft was forgotten. Here is exactly the situation with which the *Critias* was to end, described in language very like that of the Egyptian priest. The *Laws* continues the story. After the deluge came a very long and slow advance toward the present state of things. Before the metals were rediscovered there was an idyllic phase of society, resembling descriptions of the Golden Age, under the rule of patriarchal custom. Next came the beginnings of agriculture and the formation of more permanent settlements. The coalescence of various tribes led to the growth of aristocracies, or perhaps monarchies, with kings and magistrates. A third stage saw the blending of different types of constitution. Mankind, forgetting the dangers of flood, ventured down from the hills. Cities like Homer's Troy were built once more on the plains. (Here we reach what was for the Greeks the dawn of history.) Then followed the Trojan War; and the troubles consequent upon the warriors' homecoming led to the migrations. Finally we reach the settlement of Crete and Lacedaemon. The Athenian recommends a study of this succession of social forms, to discover what laws preserve a city or tend to ruin it. The history of the Dorian states suggests that government should be a mixture of monarchy and democracy. It is then proposed to apply this principle by framing laws for a new colony. Book iv opens with the choice of a site, and the rest of the treatise outlines the institutions.

Since all this fits on exactly to the end planned for the *Critias*, it may well have been Plato's original purpose to use in the *Hermocrates* the material he had been collecting from a study of the laws of Greek states. The whole trilogy would then have covered the story of the world from creation, through prehistoric legend and all historic time, to a fresh project for future reform. But Plato was getting old. The composition of the *Critias* seems to have been interrupted; it stops in an unfinished sentence. After the interruption Plato might well feel that he could not complete all this elaborate romance about the invasion from Atlantis before starting upon the subject nearest his heart, which now fills ten books of the *Laws*.[11] There was, in fact, by this time far too much material for a continuation of the *Timaeus* trilogy, even with the assistance of the unnamed absentee. So he abandoned the *Critias,* and wrote the *Laws* in place of the *Hermocrates*.[12]

[11] In the same way (*si parva licet*) Mr. H. G. Wells has, with advancing years, grown impatient of the Utopian romance and taken to expressing his hopes and fears for the future through ever thinner disguises, ending with autobiography.

[12] For the conjecture here elaborated see Raeder, 379.

# PLATO'S TIMAEUS

# TIMAEUS

## CHARACTERS OF THE DIALOGUE

SOCRATES   CRITIAS
TIMAEUS   HERMOCRATES

*Socrates.* One, two, three—but where, my dear Timaeus, is 17 the fourth of those guests of yesterday who were to entertain me today?

*Timaeus.* He suddenly felt unwell, Socrates; he would not have failed to join our company if he could have helped it.

*Socr.* Then it will fall to you and your companions to supply the part of our absent friend as well as your own.

*Tim.* By all means; we will not fail to do the best we can. b Yesterday you entertained us with the hospitality due to strangers, and it would not be fair if the rest of us were backward in offering you a feast in return.

*Socr.* Well, then, do you remember the task I set you—all the matters you were to discourse upon?

*Tim.* We can remember some; and you are here to remind us of any that we may have forgotten. Or rather, if it is not too much trouble, will you recapitulate them briefly from the beginning, to fix them more firmly in our minds?

*Socr.* I will. Yesterday the chief subject of my own dis- c course was what, as it seemed to me, would be the best form of society and the sort of men who would compose it.[1]

*Tim.* Yes, Socrates, and we all found the society you described very much to our mind.

*Socr.* We began, did we not, by separating off the farmers

[1] [The following (17c-19a) is a partial summary of *The Republic*. Cf. also the translator's Introduction—Ed.]

and all the other craftsmen from the class that was to fight in defense of the city?

*Tim.* Yes.

*Socr.* And when we assigned only one occupation to each man, one craft for which he was naturally fitted, these, we said, who were to fight on behalf of all, must be nothing else but guardians of the city against the assault of any that would injure her, whether from within or from without, dealing justice to their subjects mildly, as to natural friends, and showing a stern face to those enemies who meet them in battle.

*Tim.* Quite true.

*Socr.* There was, in fact, a certain temperament that we said a guardian should have, at once spirited and philosophic to an exceptional degree, enabling them to show a right measure of mildness or sternness to friend or foe.

*Tim.* Yes.

*Socr.* And for their education, they were to be trained in gymnastic and music and in all the studies suitable for them.

*Tim.* Certainly.

*Socr.* And the men so trained, we said, were never to regard gold or silver or anything else as their private possessions. Rather, as a garrison drawing from those whom they protect so much pay for their services as would reasonably suffice men of a temperate life, they were to share all expense and lead a common life together, in the constant exercise of manly qualities and relieved from all other occupations.

*Tim.* So it was provided.

*Socr.* And then we spoke of women. We remarked that their natures should be formed to the same harmonious blend of qualities as those of men; and they should all be given a share in men's employments of every sort, in war as well as in their general mode of life.

*Tim.* That too was prescribed.

*Socr.* And then there was the procreation of children. Here, perhaps, the novelty of our regulations makes them easy to remember. We laid down that they should all have their marriages and children in common. They were to contrive that no one of them should ever recognize his own offspring, but each should look upon all as one family, treating as brothers d and sisters all who fell within appropriate limits of age, and as parents and grandparents, or as children and grandchildren, those who fell above or below those limits.

*Tim.* Yes; that, as you say, is easy to remember.

*Socr.* Then, in order that they might have the best possible natural dispositions from birth, we said, you remember, that the magistrates of both sexes must make secret arrangements for the contraction of marriages by a certain method of draw- e ing lots, which would apportion both to the better men and to the worse partners like themselves and yet not lead to any ill-feeling, because they would imagine the allotment to be the result of chance.

*Tim.* I remember that.

*Socr.* And further, the children of the better sort were to 19 be educated, while those of the worse should be secretly dispersed through the rest of the community. The rulers were to keep the children under observation as they grew up, and from time to time take back again those who were found worthy, while the undeserving ones in their own ranks should take the places of the promoted.

*Tim.* Just so.

*Socr.* Well, then, my dear Timaeus, have we now passed in review all the main points of yesterday's conversation; or is there anything that we feel has been left out?

*Tim.* No, Socrates; you have exactly described what was b said.

*Socr.* I may now go on to tell you how I feel about the society we have described. I feel rather like a man who has been looking at some noble creatures in a painting, or perhaps at real animals, alive but motionless, and conceives a desire to watch them in motion and actively exercising the c powers promised by their form. That is just what I feel about the city we have described: I should like to hear an account of her putting forth her strength in such contests as a city will engage in against others, going to war in a manner worthy of her, and in that war achieving results befitting her training and education, both in feats of arms and in negotiation with various other states.

Now here, Critias and Hermocrates, my judgment upon myself is that to celebrate our city and its citizens as they deserve would be beyond my powers. My incapacity is not surprising; but I have formed the same judgment about the poets of the past and of today. Not that I have a low opinion of poets in general; but anyone can see that an imitator, of whatever sort, will reproduce best and most easily the surroundings in which he has been brought up; what lies outside that range is even harder to reproduce successfully in discourse than it is in action. The sophists, again, I have always thought, have had plenty of practice in making fine speeches on other subjects of all sorts; but with their habit of wandering from city to city and having no settled home of their own, I am afraid they would hardly hit upon what men who are both philosophers and statesmen would do and say in times of war, in the conduct of actual fighting or of negotiation. There remain only people of your condition, equipped by temperament and education for both philosophy and statesmanship. Timaeus, for instance, belongs to an admirably governed State, the Italian Locri,[2] where he is second to none in birth and substance, and has not only enjoyed the highest offices and distinctions his country could offer, but has also, I believe, reached the highest eminence in philosophy. Critias, again, is well known to all of us at Athens as no novice in any of the subjects we are discussing; and that Hermocrates is fully qualified in all such matters by natural gifts and education, we may trust the assurance of many witnesses. Accordingly this was in my mind yesterday when I was so ready to grant your request for a discourse on the constitution of society: I knew that, if you would consent to supply the sequel, no one could do it better; you

---

[2] The constitution of Locri was attributed to Zaleucus (Ar., *Pol.* 1274a, 22). At *Laws* 638b the Athenian says that the Locrians are reputed to have the best laws of any western state. If Timaeus never existed, this would account for Plato's choice of Locri for his native place.

could describe this city engaged in a war worthy of her and acting up to our expectations, as no other living persons could. So, after fulfilling my part, I set you, in my turn, the task of which I am now reminding you. You agreed to consult among yourselves and to requite my hospitality today. So here I am c in full dress for the entertainment, which I am most eager to receive.

*Hermocrates.* Indeed, Socrates, as Timaeus said, we shall not fail to do our best, and we have no excuse for refusing. Yesterday, as soon as we had reached Critias' guest chamber, where we are staying, and even while we were still on the way there, we were considering this very matter. Critias then produced a story which he had heard long ago. Critias, will you d repeat it now to Socrates, and he shall help us to judge whether or not it will answer the purpose of the task he is laying on us?

*Critias.* It shall be done, if our remaining partner, Timaeus, approves.

*Tim.* Certainly I approve.

*Crit.* Listen then, Socrates, to a story which, though strange, is entirely true, as Solon, wisest of the Seven,[3] once affirmed. e He was a relative and close friend of Dropides, my great-grandfather, as he says himself several times in his poems; and he told my grandfather Critias (according to the story the old

---

[3] [A name given to seven men in Ancient Greece of the period 620 to 550 B.C., who were revered for their practical wisdom and leadership. The list varies with different authorities. Plato's statement follows: "They are conscious that only a perfectly educated man is capable of uttering such expressions. Such were Thales of Miletus, and Pittacus of Mytilene, and Bias of Priene, and our own Solon, and Cleobulus of Lindus, and Myson of Chenae; and seventh in the catalogue of wise men was the Lacedaemonian Chilo. All these were lovers and emulators and disciples of the culture of the Lacedaemonians, and anyone may perceive that their wisdom was of this character, consisting of short memorable sentences, which they severally uttered. And they met together and dedicated in the temple of Apollo at Delphi, as the first fruits of their wisdom, the far-famed inscriptions which are in all men's mouths, 'Know thyself,' and 'Nothing in excess.'" Cf. *Protagoras*, 342e-343b (The Library of Liberal Arts, No. 59, p. 46)—Ed.]

man used to repeat to us) that there were great and admirable exploits performed by our own city long ago, which have been forgotten through lapse of time and the destruction of human life.[4] Greatest of all was one which it will now suit our purpose to recall, and so at once pay our debt of gratitude to you and celebrate the goddess, on her festival, with a true and merited hymn of praise.

*Socr.* Good. But what was this ancient exploit that your grandfather described on Solon's authority as unrecorded and yet really performed by our city?

*Crit.* I will tell you the story I heard as an old tale[5] from a man who was himself far from young. At that time, indeed, Critias, by his own account, was close upon ninety, and I was, perhaps, ten years old. We were keeping the Apaturia; it was the Children's Day.[6] For us boys there were the usual ceremonies: our fathers offered us prizes for reciting. Many poems by different authors were repeated, and not a few of us children sang Solon's verses, which were a novelty in those days. One of the clansmen said—either because he really thought so or to please Critias—that he considered Solon to have shown himself not only extremely wise but, in his writings, the most free-spirited of poets. The old man—how well I remember it!—was much pleased and said with a smile:

"Yes, Amynander; if only he had taken his poetry seriously like others, instead of treating it as a pastime, and if he had finished the story he brought home from Egypt and had not been forced to lay it aside by the factions and other troubles he found here on his return, I believe no other poet—not Homer or Hesiod—would have been more famous than he."

"And what was the story, Critias?" Amynander asked.

"It was about the greatest achievement ever performed by our city—one that deserved to be the most renowned of all, but

---

[4] I.e., the almost complete destructions of mankind outside Egypt by flood or fire. Both Plato and Aristotle believed that such catastrophes occur.

[5] παλαιόν, i.e., the story was already old when Critias heard it from Solon; and Critias himself was very old when he told it to his grandson.

[6] The day on which children were inscribed on the register of the clan.

through lapse of time and the destruction of the actors, the story has not lasted down to our time."

"Tell it from the beginning," said Amynander. "How and from whom did Solon hear this tale which he reported as being true?"

"In Egypt," said Critias, "at the apex of the Delta, where the stream of the Nile divides, there is a province called the Saitic. The chief city of this province is Sais, from which came King Amasis. The goddess who presides over their city is called in Egyptian Neith, in Greek, by their account, Athena; they are very friendly to Athens and claim a certain kinship with our countrymen. Solon said that, when he traveled thither, he was received with much honor; and further that, when he inquired about ancient times from the priests who knew most of such matters, he discovered that neither he nor any other Greek had any knowledge of antiquity worth speaking of. Once, wishing to lead them on to talk about ancient times, he set about telling them the most venerable of our legends, about Phoroneus the reputed first man and Niobe, and the story how Deucalion and Pyrrha survived the deluge. He traced the pedigree of their descendants, and tried, by reckoning the generations, to compute how many years had passed since those events.

" 'Ah, Solon, Solon,' said one of the priests, a very old man, 'you Greeks are always children; in Greece there is no such thing as an old man.'

" 'What do you mean?' Solon asked.

" 'You are all young in your minds,' said the priest, 'which hold no store of old belief based on long tradition, no knowledge hoary with age. The reason is this. There have been, and will be hereafter, many and divers destructions of mankind, the greatest by fire and water, though other lesser ones are due to countless other causes. Thus the story current also in your part of the world, that Phaethon, child of the Sun, once harnessed his father's chariot but could not guide it on his father's course and so burned up everything on the face of the earth and was himself consumed by the thunderbolt—this legend has the air of a fable; but the truth behind it is a deviation of the bodies that revolve in heaven round the earth and a destruction, occurring at long intervals, of things on earth by a great conflagration. At such times all who live on mountains and in high regions where it is dry perish more completely than dwellers by the rivers or the sea. We have the Nile, who preserves us in so many ways and in particular saves us from this affliction when he is set free. On the other hand, when the gods cleanse the earth with a flood of waters, the herdsmen and shepherds in the mountains are saved, while the inhabitants of cities in your part of the world are swept by the rivers into the sea. But in this country the water does not fall from above upon the fields either then or at other times; its way is always to rise up over them from below. It is for these reasons that the traditions preserved here are the oldest on record;[7] though as a matter of fact in all regions where inordinate cold or heat does not forbid it mankind exists at all times in larger or smaller numbers. Any great or noble achievement or otherwise exceptional event that has come to pass, either in your parts or here or in any place of which we have tidings, has been written down for ages past in records that are preserved in our temples; whereas with you and other peoples again and again life has only lately been enriched with letters and all the other necessaries of civilization when once more, after the usual period of years, the torrents from heaven sweep down like a pestilence leaving only the rude and unlettered among you. And so you start again like children, knowing nothing of what existed in ancient times here or in your own country. For instance, these genealogies of your countrymen, Solon, that you were reciting just now, are little better than nursery tales. To begin with, your people remember only one deluge, though there were many earlier; and moreover you do not know that the bravest and noblest race in the world once

---

[7] The Egyptian traditions are the oldest, because, although mankind is not completely destroyed anywhere, no records are kept elsewhere by the unlettered survivors of floods and conflagrations.

lived in your country. From a small remnant of their seed you and all your fellow citizens are derived; but you know nothing of it because the survivors for many generations died leaving no word in writing. Once, Solon, before the greatest of all destructions by water, what is now the city of the Athenians was the most valiant in war and in all respects the best governed beyond comparison: her exploits and her government are said to have been the noblest under heaven of which report has come to our ears.'

"On hearing this, Solon was astonished and eagerly begged the priest to tell him from beginning to end all about those ancient citizens.

"'Willingly,' answered the priest; 'I will tell you for your own sake and for your city's, and above all for honor of the goddess, patroness of our city and of yours, who has fostered both and instructed them in arts. Yours she founded first by a thousand years, from the time when she took over the seed of your people from Earth and Hephaestus; ours only in later time; and the age of our institutions is given in the sacred records as eight thousand years. Accordingly those fellow countrymen of yours lived nine thousand years ago; and I will shortly describe their laws and the noblest exploit they performed; we will go through the whole story in detail another time at our leisure, with the records before us.

"'Consider their laws in comparison with ours; you will find here today many parallels illustrating your own institutions in those days. First, there is the separation of the priesthood from the other classes; next the class of craftsmen—you will find that each kind keeps to its own craft without infringing on another; shepherds, hunters, farmers.[8] The soldiers, moreover, as you have no doubt noticed, are here distinct from all other classes; they are forbidden by law to concern themselves with anything but war. Besides, the fashion of their

---

[8] Isocrates' *Busiris* (certainly earlier in date than the *Timaeus*) mentions the Egyptian caste system, and is itself based on Herod. 2, 164-8. But it is not unlikely that Plato himself had visited Egypt.

equipment is with spear and shield, arms which we were the first people in Asia to bear, for the goddess taught us, as she had taught you first in your part of the world. Again, in the matter of wisdom, you see what great care the law has bestowed upon it here from the very beginning, both as concerns the order of the world, deriving from those divine things the discovery of all arts applied to human affairs, down to the practice of divination and medicine with a view to health, and acquiring all the other branches of learning connected therewith. All this order and system the goddess has bestowed upon you earlier when she founded your society, choosing the place in which you were born because she saw that the well-tempered climate would bear a crop of men of high intelligence. Being a lover of war and of wisdom, the goddess chose out the region that would bear men most closely resembling herself and there made her first settlement. And so you dwelt there with institutions such as I have mentioned and even better, surpassing all mankind in every excellence, as might be looked for in men born of gods and nurtured by them.

" 'Many great exploits of your city are here recorded for the admiration of all; but one surpasses the rest in greatness and valor. The records tell how great a power your city once brought to an end when it insolently advanced against all Europe and Asia, starting from the Atlantic ocean outside. For in those days that ocean could be crossed, since there was an island [9] in it in front of the strait which your countrymen tell me you call the Pillars of Heracles. The island was larger than Libya and Asia put together; and from it the voyagers of those days could reach the other islands, and from these islands the whole of the opposite continent bounding that ocean which truly deserves the name. For all these parts that lie within the strait I speak of seem to be a bay with a narrow entrance; that outer sea is the real ocean, and the land which entirely surrounds it really deserves the name of continent in

---

[9] Serious scholars now agree that Atlantis probably owed its existence entirely to Plato's imagination. See Frutiger, *Mythes de Platon*, 244 ff.

the proper sense.[10] Now on this Atlantic island there had grown up an extraordinary power under kings who ruled not only the whole island but many of the other islands and parts of the continent; and besides that, within the straits, they were lords of Libya so far as to Egypt, and of Europe to the borders of Tyrrhenia. All this power, gathered into one, attempted at one swoop to enslave your country and ours and all the region within the strait. Then it was, Solon, that the power of your city was made manifest to all mankind in its valor and strength. She was foremost of all in courage and in the arts of war, and first as the leader of Hellas, then forced by the defection of the rest to stand alone, she faced the last extreme of danger, vanquished the invaders, and set up her trophy; the peoples not yet enslaved she preserved from slavery, and all the rest of us who dwell within the bounds set by Heracles she freed with ungrudging hand. Afterwards there was time of inordinate earthquakes and floods; there came one terrible day and night, in which all your men of war were swallowed bodily by the earth, and the island Atlantis also sank beneath the sea and vanished. Hence to this day the outer ocean cannot be crossed or explored, the way being blocked by mud, just below the surface, left by the settling down of the island.' "

Now, Socrates, I have given you a brief account of the story told by the old Critias as he heard it from Solon. When you were speaking yesterday about your state and its citizens, I recalled this story and I was surprised to notice in how many points your account exactly agreed, by some miraculous chance, with Solon's. But I would say nothing at the moment; after so long an interval, my memory was imperfect. So I resolved that I would not repeat the story until I had first gone over it thoroughly in my own mind. That is why I so readily agreed to the task you laid upon us yesterday; I thought that in any case like this the hardest part is to find some suitable

---

[10] The *Etym. Mag.* connects ἤπειρος with ἄπειρος: land not bounded by sea as an island is. The outer continent is "unbounded" as forming a completely unbroken ring.

theme as a foundation for one's design, and that the need would be fairly well supplied. Accordingly, as Hermocrates has told you, no sooner had I left yesterday than I set about repeating the story to our friends as I recalled it, and when I got home I recovered pretty well the whole of it by thinking it over at night. How true is the saying that what we learn in childhood has a wonderful hold on the memory! I doubt if I could recall everything that I heard yesterday; but I should be surprised if I have lost any detail of this story told me so long ago. I listened at the time with much boyish delight, and the old man was very ready to answer the questions I kept on asking; so it has stayed in my mind indelibly like an encaustic picture. Moreover, I told it all to our friends early this morning, so that they might be as well provided as myself with materials for their discourse.

To come to the point I have been leading up to: I am ready now, Socrates, to tell the story, not in summary, but in full detail as I heard it. We will transfer the state you described yesterday and its citizens from the region of theory to concrete fact; we will take the city to be Athens and say that your imaginary citizens are those actual ancestors of ours, whom the priest spoke of. They will fit perfectly, and there will be no inconsistency in declaring them to be the real men of those ancient times. Dividing the work between us, we will all try to the best of our powers to carry out your injunctions properly. It is for you to consider, Socrates, whether this story will suit our purpose or we must look for another in its stead.

*Socr.* How could we change it for the better, Critias? Its connection with the goddess makes it specially appropriate to her festival today; and it is surely a great point that it is no fiction, but genuine history. How and where shall we find other characters, if we abandon these? No, you shall speak and good luck be with you; I have earned by my discourse of yesterday the right to take a rest and listen.

*Crit.* Then I will submit to you the plan we have arranged for your entertainment, Socrates. We decided that Timaeus shall speak first. He knows more of astronomy than the rest of us and has made knowledge of the nature of the universe his chief object; he will begin with the birth of the world and end with the nature of man. Then I am to follow, taking over from him mankind, whose origin he has described, and from you a portion of them who have received a supremely good training. I shall then, in accordance with Solon's enact-  b ment as well as with his story, bring them before our tribunal and make them our fellow citizens, on the plea that they are those old Athenians of whose disappearance we are informed by the report of the sacred writings. In the rest of our discourse we shall take their claim to the citizenship of Athens as established.

*Socr.* I see that I am to receive a complete and splendid banquet of discourse in return for mine. So you, Timaeus, are to speak next, when you have invoked the gods as custom requires.

# THE DISCOURSE OF TIMAEUS

PRELUDE: *The Nature and Scope of Physics* (27c-29d)

Timaeus' "prelude," marked off from what follows by Socrates' expression of approval (29d), lays down the principles of the whole discourse and defines the limitations of any treatment of physics. It is constructed with great care. After the opening invocation of the gods, the second paragraph states three general premises concerning anything that is not eternal, but comes to be. These premises are then applied successively to the visible universe. (1) The eternal is the intelligible; what comes to be is the sensible. Since the world is sensible, it must be a thing that comes to be. (2) Whatever comes to be must have a cause. Therefore the world has a cause—a maker and father; but he is hard to find. (3) The work of any maker will be good only if he fashions it after an eternal model. The world is good; so its model must have been eternal. Finally, the conclusion is drawn: any account that can be given of the physical world can be no better than a "likely story," because the world itself is only a "likeness" of unchanging reality.

*Tim.* That, Socrates, is what all do who have the least portion of wisdom: always, at the outset of every undertaking, small or great, they call upon a god. We who are now to discourse about the universe—how it came into being, or perhaps had no beginning of existence—must, if our senses be not altogether gone astray, invoke gods and goddesses with a prayer that our discourse throughout may be above all pleasing to them and in consequence satisfactory to us. Let this suffice, then, for our invocation of the gods; but we must also call upon our own powers, so that you may follow most readily and I may give the clearest expression to my thought on the theme proposed.

We must, then, in my judgment, first make this distinction: what is that which is always real and has no becoming, and what is that which is always becoming and is never real? That which is apprehensible by thought with a rational account is the thing that is always unchangeably real; whereas that which is the object of belief together with unreasoning sensation is the thing that becomes and passes away, but never has real being.[1] Again, all that becomes must needs become by the agency of some cause; for without a cause nothing can come to be. Now whenever the maker of anything looks to that which is always unchanging and uses a model of that description in fashioning the form and quality of his work, all that he thus accomplishes must be good.[2] If he looks to something that has come to be and uses a generated model, it will not be good.

So concerning the whole Heaven or World—let us call it by whatsoever name may be most acceptable to it[3]—we must ask the question which, it is agreed, must be asked at the outset

---

[1] Cf. the repetition of this statement below at 28b, c "as we saw, sensible things, that are to be apprehended by belief together with sensation, are things that become and can be generated."

[2] The Greek word means also "desirable," "beautiful," and will be sometimes so translated.

[3] "Heaven" (οὐρανός) is used throughout the dialogue as a synonym of *cosmos*, the entire world, not the sky.

of inquiry concerning anything: Has it always been, without any source of becoming; or has it come to be, starting from some beginning? It has come to be; for it can be seen and touched and it has body, and all such things are sensible; and, as we saw, sensible things, that are to be apprehended by belief together with sensation, are things that become and can be generated. But again, that which becomes, we say, must necessarily become by the agency of some cause. The maker and father of this universe it is a hard task to find, and having found him it would be impossible to declare him to all mankind. Be that as it may, we must go back to this question about the world: After which of the two models did its builder frame it—after that which is always in the same unchanging state, or after that which has come to be? Now if this world is good and its maker is good, clearly he looked to the eternal; on the contrary supposition (which cannot be spoken without blasphemy), to that which has come to be. Everyone, then, must see that he looked to the eternal; for the world is the best of things that have become, and he is the best of causes. Having come to be, then, in this way, the world has been fashioned on the model of that which is comprehensible by rational discourse and understanding and is always in the same state.

Again, these things being so,[4] our world must necessarily be a likeness of something. Now in every matter it is of great moment to start at the right point in accordance with the nature of the subject. Concerning a likeness, then, and its model we must make this distinction: an account is of the same order as the things which it sets forth—an account of that which is abiding and stable and discoverable by the aid of reason will itself be abiding and unchangeable (so far as it is possible and it lies in the nature of an account to be incontrovertible and irrefutable, there must be no falling short of that);[5] while an account of what is made in the image of that other, but is

[4] "These things" means the whole application to the world of the three foregoing premises.
[5] Burnet's text. The uncertainty of the reading does not affect the sense.

only a likeness, will itself be but likely, standing to accounts of the former kind in a proportion: as reality is to becoming, so is truth to belief. If then, Socrates, in many respects concerning many things—the gods and the generation of the universe—we prove unable to render an account at all points entirely consistent with itself and exact, you must not be surprised. If we can furnish accounts no less likely than any other, we must be content, remembering that I who speak and you my judges are only human, and consequently it is fitting that we should, in these matters, accept the likely story and look for nothing further.

*Socr.* Excellent, Timaeus; we must certainly accept it as you say. Your prelude we have found exceedingly acceptable; so now go on to develop your main theme.

*Plan of the Discourse.* The discourse on the nature of the universe and of man which now begins and continues without interruption to the end of the dialogue, is divided into three main sections.

(1) The first (29d-47e) is described as containing the works of Reason (τὰ διὰ Νοῦ δεδημιουργημένα, 47e), those elements in the visible world, and especially in the heavens, which most clearly manifest an intelligent and intelligible design. Here Plato approaches the world (so to say) from above, from the realm of the benevolent maker and the Forms which provide his model. The Demiurge himself is responsible for the main structure and ordered movements of the world's soul and body, and for the creation of the heavenly gods: stars, planets, and Earth. These created gods are then associated in the task of fashioning mankind and the other animals. A preliminary account of the human soul, disordered at its incarnation by the assaults of the material world, leads to the physical mechanism of sense-perception. This is contrasted with the rational purpose of sight and hearing, as revealing the order and harmony which our souls need to relearn and re-establish in themselves. The physical process whereby light acts upon the eyes or sound upon the hearing is a secondary and subordinate type of causation, the means by which the true purpose is attained. Such causation is connected with the notion of Necessity, as opposed to Reason.

(2) The second section (47e-69a) contains "what comes about of Necessity" (τὰ δι' Ἀνάγκης γιγνόμενα, 47e). Making a fresh start, the discourse plunges into the obscure region of the bodily and of blind causation, approaching the world this time from below. A new factor, Space, is introduced, as the necessary condition or medium in which Becoming images reality. The unlimited and unordered qualities and powers of the bodily are pictured as a chaos. The Demiurge imposes upon them a rational element of geometrical form in the shapes of the four primary bodies. The properties of these regular figures are then connected with certain qualities in the sensations we receive; and so, from the opposite pole, we return to the point of contact between the human organism and the outer world, where the first part ended.

(3) In the third section (69a-end), the two strands of rational purpose and necessity are woven together in a more detailed account of the human frame, the working of its organs, and the disorders of body and soul.

## I. THE WORKS OF REASON

### *The motive of creation* (29d-30c)

*Tim.* Let us, then, state for what reason becoming and this universe were framed by him who framed them. He was good; and in the good no jealousy in any matter can ever arise. So, being without jealousy, he desired that all things should come as near as possible to being like himself. That this is the supremely valid principle of becoming and of the order of the world, we shall most surely be right to accept from men of understanding. Desiring, then, that all things should be good and, so far as might be, nothing imperfect, the god took over all that is visible—not at rest, but in discordant and unordered motion—and brought it from disorder into order, since he judged that order was in every way the better.

Now it was not, nor can it ever be, permitted that the work of the supremely good should be anything but that which is best. Taking thought, therefore, he found that, among things that are by nature visible, no work that is without intelligence will ever be better than one that has intelligence, when each is taken as a whole, and moreover that intelligence cannot be present in anything apart from soul. In virtue of this reasoning, when he framed the universe, he fashioned reason within soul and soul within body, to the end that the work he accomplished might be by nature as excellent and perfect as possible. This, then, is how we must say, according to the likely account, that this world came to be, by the god's providence, in very truth [1] a living creature with soul and reason.

### *The creator's model* (30c-31a)

This being premised, we have now to state what follows next: What was the living creature in whose likeness he framed the world? We must not suppose that it was any creature that ranks only as a species; for no copy of that which is incomplete can ever be good. Let us rather say that the world is like, above all things, to that Living Creature of which all other living creatures, severally and in their families, are parts. For that embraces and contains within itself all the intelligible living creatures, just as this world contains ourselves and all other creatures that have been formed as things visible. For the god, wishing to make this world most nearly like that intelligible thing which is best and in every way complete, fashioned it as a single visible living creature, containing within itself all living things whose nature is of the same order.

### *One world, not many* (31a-b)

Have we, then, been right to call it one Heaven, or would it have been true rather to speak of many and indeed of an indefinite number? One we must call it, if we are to hold that it was made according to its pattern. For that which embraces all the intelligible living creatures that there are, cannot be one of a pair; for then there would have to be yet another

---

[1] It is literally true (not merely "probable") that the world is an intelligent living creature.

Living Creature embracing those two, and they would be parts of it; and thus our world would be more truly described as a likeness, not of them, but of that other which would embrace them. Accordingly, to the end that this world may be like the complete Living Creature in respect of its uniqueness, for that reason its maker did not make two worlds nor yet an indefinite number; but this Heaven has come to be and is and shall be hereafter one and unique.

### THE BODY OF THE WORLD

*Why this consists of four primary bodies* (31b-32c)

Now that which comes to be must be bodily, and so visible and tangible; and nothing can be visible without fire, or tangible without something solid,[1] and nothing is solid without earth. Hence the god, when he began to put together the body of the universe, set about making it of fire and earth. But two things alone cannot be satisfactorily united without a third; for there must be some bond between them drawing them together. And of all bonds the best is that which makes itself and the terms it connects a unity in the fullest sense; and it is of the nature of a continued geometrical proportion to effect this most perfectly. For whenever, of three numbers, the middle one between any two that are either solids (cubes?) or squares is such that, as the first is to it, so is it to the last, and conversely as the last is to the middle, so is the middle to the first, then since the middle becomes first and last, and again the last and first become middle, in that way all will necessarily come to play the same part toward one another, and by so doing they will all make a unity.

Now if it had been required that the body of the universe should be a plane surface with no depth, a single mean would have been enough to connect its companions and itself; but in fact the world was to be solid in form, and solids are always

---

[1] Solid, i.e., resistant to touch (Pr. ii, 12²¹).

conjoined, not by one mean, but by two. Accordingly the god set water and air between fire and earth, and made them, so far as was possible, proportional to one another, so that as fire is to air, so is air to water, and as air is to water, so is water to earth, and thus he bound together the frame of a world visible and tangible.

For these reasons and from such constituents, four in number, the body of the universe was brought into being, coming into concord by means of proportion, and from these it acquired Amity, so that coming into unity with itself it became indissoluble by any other save him who bound it together.

### *The world's body contains the whole of all the four primary bodies* (32c-33b)

Now the frame of the world took up the whole of each of these four; he who put it together made it consist of all the fire and water and air and earth, leaving no part or power of any one of them outside. This was his intent: first, that it might be in the fullest measure a living being whole and complete, of complete parts; next, that it might be single, nothing being left over, out of which such another might come into being; and moreover that it might be free from age and sickness. For he perceived that, if a body be composite, when hot things and cold and all things that have strong powers beset that body and attack it from without, they bring it to untimely dissolution and cause it to waste away by bringing upon it sickness and age. For this reason and so considering, he fashioned it as a single whole consisting of all these wholes, complete and free from age and sickness.

### *It is a sphere, without organs or limbs, rotating on its axis* (33b-34a)

And for shape he gave it that which is fitting and akin to its nature. For the living creature that was to embrace all living creatures within itself, the fitting shape would be the figure that comprehends in itself all the figures there are; accordingly, he turned its shape rounded and spherical, equidistant every way from center to extremity—a figure the most perfect and uniform of all; for he judged uniformity to be immeasurably better than its opposite. And all round on the outside he made it perfectly smooth, for several reasons. It had no need of eyes, for nothing visible was left outside; nor of hearing, for there was nothing outside to be heard. There was no surrounding air to require breathing, nor yet was it in need of any organ by which to receive food into itself or to discharge it again when drained of its juices. For nothing went out or came into it from anywhere, since there was nothing: it was designed to feed itself on its own waste and to act and be acted upon entirely by itself and within itself; because its framer thought that it would be better self-sufficient, rather than dependent upon anything else.

It had no need of hands to grasp with or to defend itself, nor yet of feet or anything that would serve to stand upon; so he saw no need to attach to it these limbs to no purpose. For he assigned to it the motion proper to its bodily form, namely, that one of the seven which above all belongs to reason and intelligence; accordingly, he caused it to turn about uniformly in the same place and within its own limits and made it revolve round and round; he took from it all the other six motions and gave it no part in their wanderings. And since for this revolution it needed no feet, he made it without feet or legs.

## THE WORLD-SOUL

### Summary. Transition to the World-Soul (34a-b)

All this, then, was the plan of the god who is forever for the god who was sometime to be. According to this plan he made it smooth and uniform, everywhere equidistant from its center, a body whole and complete, with complete bodies for its parts. And in the center he set a soul and caused it to extend throughout the whole and further wrapped its body round with soul on the outside; and so he established one world alone, round and revolving in a circle, solitary but able by reason of its excellence to bear itself company, needing no other acquaintance or friend but sufficient to itself. On all these accounts the world which he brought into being was a blessed god.

### *Soul is prior to body* (34b-c)

Now this soul, though it comes later in the account we are now attempting, was not made by the god younger than the body; for when he joined them together, he would not have suffered the elder to be ruled by the younger. There is in us too much of the casual and random,[1] which shows itself in our speech; but the god made soul prior to body and more venerable in birth and excellence, to be the body's mistress and governor.

### *Composition of the World-Soul* (35a)

The things of which he composed soul and the manner of its composition were as follows: (1) Between the indivisible Existence that is ever in the same state and the divisible Existence that becomes in bodies, he compounded a third form of Existence composed of both. (2) Again, in the case of Sameness and in that of Difference, he also on the same principle made a compound intermediate between that kind of them which is indivisible and the kind that is divisible in bodies. (3) Then, taking the three, he blended them all into a unity, forcing the nature of Difference, hard as it was to mingle, into union with Sameness, and mixing them together with Existence.[2]

[1] Because we are not wholly rational, but partly subject to those wandering causes which, "being destitute of reason, produce their sundry effects at random and without order" (46e).

[2] The sentence (which, for convenience, I have divided into three numbered parts) is one of the most obscure in the whole dialogue, but not so obscure as it has been made by critics, who have altered the text and thereby dislocated the grammar and the sense. The sentence falls into three

*Division of the World-Soul into harmonic intervals*
(35b-36b)

And having made a unity of the three, again he divided this whole into as many parts as was fitting, each part being a blend of Sameness, Difference, and Existence. b

And he began the division in this way. First he took one portion (1) from the whole, and next a portion (2) double of this; the third (3) half as much again as the second, and three times the first; the fourth (4) double of the second; the fifth (9) three times the third; the sixth (8) eight times the first; [3] and the seventh (27) twenty-seven times the first. c

---

clauses: (1) The first describes the compounding, out of indivisible, unchanging Existence and the divisible Existence which becomes in the region of the bodily, of a third kind of Existence intermediate between them. This intermediate sort of Existence is one of the three ingredients in the final mixture of the last clause. (2) The second clause states that the Demiurge proceeded on the same principle (κατὰ ταὐτά) also in the case of Sameness and in that of Difference. As there were two kinds of Existence, the indivisible and the divisible, so Sameness and Difference have each two corresponding kinds, described as "that kind of them which is indivisible, and the kind that is divisible in bodies." Accordingly, as before, the Demiurge made a third intermediate kind of Sameness (and again of Difference), composed of the indivisible and divisible kinds of Sameness (and of Difference). These intermediate kinds of Sameness and of Difference are the second and third ingredients in the final mixture. (3) Finally, taking the three ingredients, the Demiurge mixes them all into a unity. We may set out the full scheme of the Soul's composition as follows:

|  | First Mixture | | Final Mixture |
|---|---|---|---|
| Indivisible Existence<br>Divisible Existence | } | Intermediate Existence | }  |
| Indivisible Sameness<br>Divisible Sameness | } | Intermediate Sameness | } Soul |
| Indivisible Difference<br>Divisible Difference | } | Intermediate Difference | } |

[3] 9 precedes 8, "because 9 is a lower power, being the square of 3, while 8 is the cube of 2" A.-H., *ad loc.*).

**36** Next, he went on to fill up both the double and the triple intervals, cutting off yet more parts from the original mixture and placing them between the terms, so that within each interval there were two means, the one (harmonic) exceeding the one extreme and being exceeded by the other by the same fraction of the extremes, the other (arithmetic) exceeding the one extreme by the same number whereby it was exceeded by the other.[4]

These links gave rise to intervals of $\frac{3}{2}$ and $\frac{4}{3}$ and $\frac{9}{8}$ within the original intervals.[5]

**b** And he went on to fill up all the intervals of $\frac{4}{3}$ (i.e., fourths) with the interval $\frac{9}{8}$ (the tone), leaving over in each a fraction.

---

[4] If we take for illustration the extremes 6 and 12, the harmonic mean is 8, exceeding the one extreme (6) by one-third of 6 and exceeded by the other extreme (12) by one-third of 12. The arithmetic mean is 9, exceeding 6 and falling short of 12 by the same number, 3.

[5] When we insert the harmonic and arithmetical means between each two successive terms of the original series, we obtain:

$$1 \quad \frac{4}{3} \quad \frac{3}{2} \quad 2 \quad \frac{8}{3} \quad [3] \quad 4 \quad \frac{16}{3} \quad 6 \quad 8$$

$$1 \quad \left[\frac{3}{2}\right] \quad [2] \quad 3 \quad \frac{9}{2} \quad [6] \quad 9 \quad \frac{27}{2} \quad 18 \quad 27$$

Omitting the numbers in brackets, which occur in both series, we obtain the single series:

$$1 \quad \frac{4}{3} \quad \frac{3}{2} \quad 2 \quad \frac{8}{3} \quad 3 \quad 4 \quad \frac{9}{2} \quad \frac{16}{3} \quad 6 \quad 8 \quad 9 \quad \frac{27}{2} \quad 18 \quad 27$$

If we now fill in the corresponding notes, the result is as follows:

As the last sentence remarks, this "gives rise to intervals of a fifth $\left(\frac{3}{2}\right)$ or a fourth $\left(\frac{4}{3}\right)$ or a tone $\left(\frac{9}{8}\right)$ within the original intervals." The final step, taken in the next sentence, is to fill up every tetrachord with two intervals of a tone $\left(\frac{9}{8}\right)$ and a remainder $\left(\frac{256}{243}\right)$ nearly equivalent to our semitone.

This remaining interval of the fraction had its terms in the numerical proportion of 256 to 243 (semitone).

By this time the mixture from which he was cutting off these portions was all used up.

### Construction of the Circles of the Same and the Different and the planetary circles (36b-d)

This whole fabric, then, he split lengthwise into two halves; and making the two cross one another at their centers in the form of the letter X, he bent each round into a circle and joined it up, making each meet itself and the other at a point opposite to that where they had been brought into contact.

He then comprehended them in the motion that is carried round uniformly in the same place, and made the one the outer, the other the inner circle. The outer movement he named the movement of the Same; the inner, the movement of the Different. The movement of the Same he caused to revolve to the right by way of the side; the movement of the Different to the left by way of the diagonal.

And he gave the supremacy to the revolution of the Same and uniform; for he left that single and undivided; but the inner revolution he split in six places into seven unequal circles, severally corresponding with the double and triple intervals, of each of which there were three. And he appointed that the circles should move in opposite senses to one another; while in speed three should be similar, but the other four should differ in speed from one another and from the three, though moving according to ratio.

### The world's body fitted to its soul (36d-e)

When the whole fabric of the soul had been finished to its maker's mind, he next began to fashion within the soul all that is bodily, and brought the two together, fitting them center to center. And the soul, being everywhere inwoven from the center to the outermost heaven and enveloping the heaven all round on the outside, revolving within its own limit, made a divine beginning of ceaseless and intelligent life for all time.

## Discourse in the World-Soul (36e-37c)

Now the body of the heaven has been created visible; but she is invisible, and, as a soul having part in reason and harmony, is the best of things brought into being by the most excellent of things intelligible and eternal. Seeing, then, that soul had been blended of Sameness, Difference, and Existence, these three portions, and had been in due proportion divided and bound together, and moreover revolves upon herself, whenever she is in contact with anything that has dispersed existence or with anything whose existence is indivisible, she is set in motion all through herself and tells in what respect precisely, and how, and in what sense, and when, it comes about that something is qualified as either the same or different with respect to any given thing, whatever it may be, with which it is the same or from which it differs, either in the sphere of things that become or with regard to things that are always changeless.

Now whenever discourse that is alike true, whether it takes place concerning that which is different or that which is the same, being carried on without speech or sound within the thing that is self-moved,[6] is about that which is sensible, and the circle of the Different, moving aright, carries its message throughout all its soul—then there arise judgments and beliefs that are sure and true. But whenever discourse is concerned with the rational, and the circle of the Same, running smoothly, declares it, the result must be rational understanding and knowledge. And if anyone calls that in which this

---

[6] The self-moved thing is the Heaven as a whole, which, as a living creature, is self-moved by its own self-moving soul. That an animal (soul and body) is self-moved is a commonplace. Ar., *Phys.* 265*b*, 34. "Witness to this truth (that locomotion is prior to other motions) is borne by those who make soul the cause of motion, for they say that what moves itself is the source of motion and the *animal or anything that has a soul does move itself locally.*"

pair [7] come to exist by any name but "soul," his words will be anything rather than the truth.

### *Time, the moving likeness of Eternity* (37c-38c)

When the father who had begotten it saw it set in motion and alive, a shrine brought into being for the everlasting gods, he rejoiced and being well pleased he took thought to make it yet more like its pattern. So as that pattern is the Living Being that is forever existent, he sought to make this universe also like it, so far as might be, in that respect. Now the nature of that Living Being was eternal, and this character it was impossible to confer in full completeness on the generated thing. But he took thought to make, as it were, a moving likeness of eternity; and, at the same time that he ordered the Heaven, he made, of eternity that abides in unity, an everlasting likeness moving according to number—that to which we have given the name Time.

For there were no days and nights, months and years, before the Heaven came into being; but he planned that they should now come to be at the same time that the Heaven was framed. All these are parts of Time, and "was" and "shall be" are forms of time that have come to be; we are wrong to transfer them unthinkingly to eternal being. We say that it was and is and shall be; but "is" alone really belongs to it and describes it truly; "was" and "shall be" are properly used of becoming which proceeds in time, for they are motions. But that which is forever in the same state immovably cannot be becoming older or younger by lapse of time, nor can it ever become so; neither can it now have been, nor will it be in the future; and in general nothing belongs to it of all that Becoming attaches to the moving things of sense; but these have come into being as forms of time, which images eternity and

---

[7] I incline to think (with A.-H.) that "this pair" means rational understanding and knowledge, because Plato thinks it worth while repeatedly to assert that νοῦς can exist only in soul (30b, 46d, *Soph.* 249a, *Philebus*, 30c), though the same is true of judgments and beliefs.

revolves according to number. And besides we make statements like these: that what is past *is* past, what happens now *is* happening now, and again that what will happen *is* what will happen, and that the nonexistent *is* nonexistent: no one of these expressions is exact. But this, perhaps, may not be the right moment for a precise discussion of these matters.

Be that as it may, Time came into being together with the Heaven, in order that, as they were brought into being together, so they may be dissolved together, if ever their dissolution should come to pass; and it is made after the pattern of the ever-enduring nature, in order that it may be as like that pattern as possible; for the pattern is a thing that has being for all eternity, whereas the Heaven has been and is and shall be perpetually throughout all time.

### *The Planets as instruments of Time* (38c-39e)

In virtue, then, of this plan and intent of the god for the birth of Time, in order that Time might be brought into being, Sun and Moon and five other stars—"wanderers," as they are called—were made to define and preserve the numbers of Time. Having made a body for each of them, the god set them in the circuits in which the revolution of the Different was moving—in seven circuits seven bodies: the Moon in the circle nearest the Earth; the Sun in the second above the Earth; the Morning Star (Venus) and the one called sacred to Hermes (Mercury) in circles revolving so as, in point of speed, to run their race with the Sun, but possessing the power contrary to his; whereby the Sun and the star of Hermes and the Morning Star alike overtake and are overtaken by one another. As for the remainder, where he enshrined them and for what reasons—if one should explain all these, the account, though only by the way, would be a heavier task than that for the sake of which it was given. Perhaps these things may be duly set forth later at our leisure.

To resume: when each one of the beings that were to join in producing Time had come into the motion suitable to it, and, as bodies bound together with living bonds, they had become living creatures and learned their appointed task,[8] then they began to revolve by way of the motion of the Different, which was aslant, crossing the movement of the Same and subject to it: some moving in greater circles, some in lesser; those in the lesser circles moving faster, those in the greater more slowly.

So, by reason of the movement of the Same, those which revolve most quickly appeared to be overtaken by the slower, though really overtaking them. For the movement of the Same, which gives all their circles a spiral twist because they have two distinct forward motions in opposite senses, made the body which departs most slowly from itself—the swiftest of all movements—appear as keeping pace with it most closely.

And in order that there might be a conspicuous measure for the relative speed and slowness with which they moved in their eight revolutions, the god kindled a light in the second orbit from the Earth—what we now call the Sun—in order that he might fill the whole heaven with his shining and that all living things for whom it was meet might possess number, learning it from the revolution of the Same and uniform. Thus and for these reasons day and night came into being, the period of the single and most intelligent revolution.[9]

The month comes to be when the Moon completes her own circle and overtakes the Sun; the year, when the Sun has gone round his own circle. The periods of the rest have not been observed by men, save for a few; and men have no names for them, nor do they measure one against another by numerical reckoning. They barely know that the wanderings of these others are time at all, bewildering as they are in number and of surprisingly intricate pattern. Nonetheless it is possible to grasp that the perfect number of time fulfills the perfect year

---

[8] Here, as at *Laws* 898, it is clearly stated that every planet, like the other heavenly gods, is a living creature with a body and an intelligent soul.

[9] The single (undivided) revolution of the same, which is the only motion of translation possessed by the fixed stars.

at the moment when the relative speeds of all the eight revolutions have accomplished their courses together and reached their consummation, as measured by the circle of the Same and uniformly moving.

In this way, then, and for these ends were brought into being all those stars that have turnings on their journey through the Heaven; in order that this world may be as like as possible to the perfect and intelligible Living Creature, in respect of imitating its ever-enduring nature.

### *The four kinds of living creature. The heavenly gods*
### (39e-40b)

Now so far, up to the birth of Time, the world had been made in other respects in the likeness of its pattern; but it was still unlike in that it did not yet contain all living creatures brought into being within it. So he set about accomplishing this remainder of his work, making the copy after the nature of the model. He thought that this world must possess all the different forms that intelligence discerns contained in the Living Creature that truly is. And there are four: one, the heavenly race of gods; second, winged things whose path is in the air; third, all that dwells in the water; and fourth, all that goes on foot on the dry land.

The form of the divine kind he made for the most part of fire, that it might be most bright and fair to see; and after the likeness of the universe he gave them well-rounded shape, and set them in the intelligence of the supreme to keep company with it, distributing them all round the heaven, to be in very truth an adornment (*cosmos*) for it, embroidered over the whole. And he assigned to each two motions: one uniform in the same place, as each always thinks the same thoughts about the same things; the other a forward motion, as each is subjected to the revolution of the Same and uniform. But in respect of the other five motions he made each motionless and still, in order that each might be as perfect as possible.

For this reason came into being all the unwandering stars,

living beings divine and everlasting, which abide forever revolving uniformly upon themselves; while those stars that having turnings and in that sense "wander" came to be in the manner already described.

### Rotation of the Earth (40b-c)

And Earth he designed to be at once our nurse and, as she winds round the axis that stretches right through, the guardian and maker of night and day, first and most venerable of all the gods that are within the heaven.

### The further movements of the heavenly bodies are too complicated for description here (40c-d)

To describe the evolutions in the dance of these same gods, their juxtapositions, the counterrevolutions of their circles relatively to one another, and their advances; to tell which of the gods come into line with one another at their conjunctions, and which in opposition, and in what order they pass in front of or behind one another, and at what periods of time they are severally hidden from our sight and again reappearing send to men who cannot calculate panic fears and signs of things to come—to describe all this without visible models of these same would be labor spent in vain. So this much shall suffice on this head, and here let our account of the nature of the visible and generated gods come to an end.

With this conclusion Plato breaks off his account of the motions of the heavenly gods. It will be convenient here to give a table of all the celestial motions mentioned in the *Timaeus*.

### TABLE OF CELESTIAL MOTIONS

A. MOTIONS OF THE WHOLE

*Self-motions of the World-Soul:*

(1) The Same (37c), imparted as axial rotation to

the whole spherical body from center to circumference (34a, b, 36e).

(2) The Different, a single motion (36c, 37b, 38c), imparted to the planets (only) by distribution among seven circles (36c, d).

B. MOTIONS OF PARTS:

(a) *Individual Stars:*

(1) The Same, imparted to each star as a "forward" motion of diurnal revolution (40b).

(2) Self-motion: axial rotation (40a).

(b) *The Seven Planets:*

(1) The Same, imparted to each planet by the "supremacy" of the Same (36c, 39a).

(2) The Different, imparted to each planet as a constituent of its proper motion on a circular track (the seven circles, 36c, d).

The composition of these two motions results in the Spiral Twist (39a).

(3) Self-motions:

(α) Axial rotation of each planet (implied at 40a, b).

(β) Differences of speed of the several planets (36d): The Moon accelerates the movement of the Different. The Sun, Venus, Mercury, as a group, move with the actual speed of the Different, completing their course in a year. The Sun alone has the actual motion of the Different unmodified; Venus and Mercury modify it by intermittent retrogradation (38d). Mars, Jupiter, Saturn slow down the movement of the Different by an additional motion of counter-revolution (ἐπανακύκλησις 40c). These are the three circles with a motion contrary to the Different and to the remaining four (36d).

(γ) Retrogradation of all planets, except Sun and Moon: This is the "contrary tendency" (ἐναντία δύναμις, 38d) explicitly ascribed to Venus and Mercury, but also shared by Mars, Jupiter, Saturn. It involves variations in the speed of each planet, and intermittent counter-revolution accelerated to the point of bringing the main motion to a stand and temporarily reversing its sense.

(None of these self-motions distorts in any way the circular track of the planet's proper motion. So the planets do not "stray" from one path to another, *Laws* 821, *Epin.* 982c.)

(*c*) *Earth:*
   (1) The Same, imparted to Earth as part of the whole body of the world rotating on its axis (34a, 36e).
   (2) Self-motion: axial rotation at the center, relatively to the fixed stars, counteracting the imparted motion of the Same (40b).

THE HUMAN SOUL AND BODY

*The traditional Gods* (40d-41a)

As concerning the other divinities, to know and to declare their generation is too high a task for us; we must trust those who have declared it in former times: being, as they said, descendants of gods, they must, no doubt, have had certain knowledge of their own ancestors. We cannot, then, mistrust the children of gods, though they speak without probable or necessary proofs; when they profess to report their family history, we must follow established usage and accept what they say. Let us, then, take on their word this account of the generation of these gods. As children of Earth and Heaven were born Oceanus and Tethys; and of these Phorkys and Cronos and Rhea and all their company; and of Cronos and Rhea, Zeus and Hera and all their brothers and sisters whose names we know; and of these yet other offspring.

## *The address to the gods* (41a-d)

Be that as it may, when all the gods had come to birth—both all that revolve before our eyes and all that reveal themselves in so far as they will—the author of this universe addressed them in these words:

"Gods,[1] of gods whereof I am the maker and of works the father, those which are my own handiwork are indissoluble, save with my consent. Now, although whatsoever bond[2] has been fastened may be unloosed, yet only an evil will could consent to dissolve what has been well fitted together and is in a good state; therefore, although you, having come into being, are not immortal nor indissoluble altogether, nevertheless you shall not be dissolved nor taste of death, finding my will a bond yet stronger and more sovereign than those wherewith you were bound together when you came to be.

"Now, therefore, take heed to this that I declare to you. There are yet left mortal creatures of three kinds that have not been brought into being. If these be not born, the Heaven will be imperfect; for it will not contain all the kinds of living being, as it must if it is to be perfect and complete. But if I myself gave them birth and life, they would be equal to gods. In order, then, that mortal things may exist and this All may be truly all, turn according to your own nature to the making of living creatures, imitating my power in generating you. In so far as it is fitting that something in them should share the name of the immortals, being called divine and ruling over those among them who at any time are willing to follow after righteousness and after you—that part, having sown it as seed and made a beginning, I will hand over to

---

[1] If the slight correction I have proposed in the first sentence of this address be accepted, the sense is satisfactory. "Gods and works whereof I am father and maker" means the whole universe, of which the Demiurge has been called maker and father at 28c.

[2] The "living bonds" connecting the souls and bodies of the celestial gods, mentioned at 38e.

you. For the rest, do you, weaving mortal to immortal, make living beings; bring them to birth, feed them, and cause them to grow; and when they fail, receive them back again."

*The Composition of human souls. The Laws of Destiny*
*(41d-42d)*

Having said this, he turned once more to the same mixing bowl wherein he had mixed and blended the soul of the universe, and poured into it what was left of the former ingredients, blending them this time in somewhat the same way, only no longer so pure as before, but second or third in degree of purity. And when he had compounded the whole, he divided it into souls equal in number with the stars, and distributed them, each soul to its several star. There mounting them as it were in chariots, he showed them the nature of the universe and declared to them the laws of Destiny. There would be appointed a first incarnation one and the same for all, that none might suffer disadvantage at his hands; and they were to be sown into the instruments of time, each one into that which was meet for it, and to be born as the most godfearing of living creatures; and human nature being twofold, the better sort was that which should thereafter be called "man."

Whensoever, therefore, they should of necessity have been implanted in bodies, and of their bodies some part should always be coming in and some part passing out, there must needs be innate in them, first, sensation, the same for all, arising from violent impressions; second, desire blended with pleasure and pain, and besides these fear and anger and all the feelings that accompany these and all that are of a contrary nature: and if they should master these passions, they would live in righteousness; if they were mastered by them, in unrighteousness.

And he who should live well for his due span of time should journey back to the habitation of his consort star and there live a happy and congenial life; but failing of this, he

should shift at his second birth into a woman; and if in this
condition he still did not cease from wickedness, then according to the character of his depravation, he should constantly be changed into some beast of a nature resembling the formation of that character, and should have no rest from the travail of these changes, until letting the revolution of the Same and uniform within himself draw into its train all that turmoil or fire and water and air and earth that had later grown about it, he should control its irrational turbulence by discourse of reason and return once more to the form of his first and best condition.

### *Human souls sown in Earth and the planets* (42d-e)

When he had delivered to them all these ordinances, to the end that he might be guiltless of the future wickedness of any one of them, he sowed them, some in the Earth, some in the Moon, some in all the other instruments of time. After this sowing he left it to the newly made gods to mold mortal bodies, to fashion all that part of a human soul that there was still need to add and all that these things entail, and to govern and guide the mortal creature to the best of their powers, save in so far as it should be a cause of evil to itself.

### *The condition of the soul when newly incarnated*
### (42e-44d)

When he had made all these dispositions, he continued to abide by the wont of his own nature; and meanwhile his sons took heed to their father's ordinance and set about obeying it. Having received the immortal principle of a mortal creature, imitating their own maker, they borrowed from the world portions of fire and earth, water and air, on condition that these loans should be repaid, and cemented together what they took, not with the indissoluble bonds whereby they were themselves held together, but welding them with a multitude of rivets too small to be seen and so making each body a unity of all the portions. And they confined the circuits of the immortal soul within the flowing and ebbing tide of the body.

These circuits, being thus confined in a strong river, neither controlled it nor were controlled, but caused and suffered violent motions; so that the whole creature moved, but advanced at hazard without order or method, having all the six motions; for they went forward and backward, and again to right and left, and up and down, straying every way in all the six directions. For strong as was the tide that brought them nourishment, flooding them and ebbing away, a yet greater tumult was caused by the qualities of the things that assailed them, when some creature's body chanced to encounter alien fire from outside, or solid concretion of earth and softly gliding waters, or was overtaken by the blast of air-borne winds, and the motions caused by all these things passed through the body to the soul and assailed it. (For this reason these motions were later called by the name they still bear—"sensations.") And so at the moment we speak of, causing for the time being a strong and widespread commotion and joining with that perpetually streaming current in stirring and violently shaking the circuits of the soul, they completely hampered the revolution of the Same by flowing counter to it and stopped it from going on its way and governing; and they dislocated the revolution of the Different. Accordingly, the intervals of the double and the triple,[3] three of each sort, and the connecting means of the ratios, $\frac{3}{2}$ and $\frac{4}{3}$ and $\frac{9}{8}$, since they could not be completely dissolved save by him who bound them together, were twisted by them in all manner of ways, and all possible infractions and deformations of the circles were caused; so that they barely held together, and though they moved, their motion was unregulated, now reversed, now sidelong, now inverted. It was as when a man stands on his

---

[3] The first mention of the harmonic intervals as present in the individual soul. They stand for that harmony and κοσμιότης which need to be re-established by contemplation of the kindred harmony of the World Soul, revealed in the heavenly revolutions (47c).

head, resting it on the earth, and holds his feet aloft by thrusting them against something: in such a case right and left both of the man and of the spectators appear reversed to the other party. The same and similar effects are produced with great intensity in the soul's revolutions; and when they meet with something outside that falls under the Same or the Different, they speak of it as the same as this or different from that contrary to the true facts, and show themselves mistaken and foolish. Also [4] at such times no one revolution among their number is acting as governor or guide; but whatever revolutions are assailed by certain sensations coming from without, which draw in their train at the same time the whole vessel of the soul, at such times only seem to be in control, whereas really they are overpowered. It is, indeed, because of these affections that today, as in the beginning, a soul comes to be without intelligence at first, when it is bound in a mortal body.[5]

But when the current of growth and nutriment flows in less strongly, and the revolutions, taking advantage of the calm, once more go their own way and become yet more settled as time goes on, thenceforward the revolutions are corrected to the form that belongs to the several circles in their natural motion; and giving their right names to what is different and to what is the same, they set their possessor in the way to become rational. And now if some right nurture lends help toward education,[6] he becomes entirely whole and un-

---

[4] This clause goes with what follows; it refers to lack of control over behavior. An infant's earliest actions are determined not by judgment or thought or will, but mechanically by "motions" of sensation rushing in from without and sweeping with them the motions of the soul. Its behavior only looks like voluntary self-motion.

[5] The whole description applies to every newborn baby's soul, not only to the first generation of mankind. Contrast the World Soul which, as soon as it was joined with its body, began an "*intelligent* life" (ἔμφρων βίος, 36e), not being exposed to external assaults.

[6] Cf. 47c: the observation of the unperturbed revolutions of the heavens will lead to philosophy, and we shall learn to "reproduce the perfectly unerring (ἀπλανεῖς) revolutions of the god (the Heaven) and reduce to

blemished, having escaped the worst of maladies; whereas if c
he be neglectful, he journeys through a life halt and maimed
and comes back to Hades uninitiate and without understanding.

These things, however, come to pass at a later stage. Our
present subject must be treated in more detail; and its preliminaries, concerning the generation of bodies, part by part,
and concerning soul, and the reasons and forethought of the
gods in producing them—of all this we must go on to tell, on
the principle of holding fast to the most likely account.  d

*Structure of the human body: head and limbs*
(44d-45b)

Copying the round shape of the universe, they confined
the two divine revolutions in a spherical body—the head, as
we now call it—which is the divinest part of us and lord over
all the rest. To this the gods gave the whole body, when they
had assembled it, for its service, perceiving that it possessed
all the motions that were to be.[7] Accordingly, that the head
might not roll upon the ground with its heights and hollows
of all sorts, and have no means to surmount the one or to  e
climb out of the other, they gave it the body as a vehicle for
ease of travel; that is why the body is elongated and grew
four limbs that can be stretched out or bent, the god contriving thus for its traveling. Clinging and supporting itself
with these limbs, it is able to make its way through every
region,[8] carrying at the top of us the habitation of the most 45
divine and sacred part. Thus and for these reasons legs and

---

settled order the wandering (πλανωμένας) motions in ourselves." Cf. 90d
and 87b.

[7] The bodies of the universe and of the created gods possessed only rotation and orbital revolution—the rational motions. Inferior creatures have all the six rectilinear motions proper to the primary bodies, portions of which are "assembled" to compose their bodies.

[8] The six regions (τόποι) of 43b, answering to the six motions (34a) "up and down," "forward and backward," "right and left," which the World's body has not.

arms grow upon us all. And the gods, holding that the front is more honorable and fit to lead than the back, gave us movement for the most part in that direction. So man must needs have the front of the body distinguished and unlike the back; so first they set the face on the globe of the head on that side and fixed in it organs for all the forethought of the soul, and appointed this, our natural front, to be the part having leadership.

### The eyes and the mechanism of vision (45b-46a)

First of the organs they fabricated the eyes to bring us light, and fastened them there for the reason which I will now describe. Such fire as has the property, not of burning, but of yielding a gentle light, they contrived should become the proper body of each day. For [9] the pure fire within us is akin to this, and they caused it to flow through the eyes, making the whole fabric of the eyeball, and especially the central part (the pupil), smooth and close in texture,[10] so as to let nothing pass that is of coarser stuff, but only fire of this description to filter through pure by itself. Accordingly, whenever there is daylight round about, the visual current issues forth, like to like, and coalesces with it and is formed into a single homogeneous body in a direct line with the eyes, in whatever quarter the stream issuing from within strikes upon any object it encounters outside. So the whole, because of its homogeneity, is similarly affected and passes on the motions of anything it comes in contact with or that comes into contact with it, throughout the whole body, to the soul, and thus causes the sensation we call seeing.

[9] The connection of thought ("for") is: the gods made daylight (essentially a visible thing) of a suitable kind of fire, *for* they wanted us to see and so arranged that the fire within the eye should be similar and capable of coalescing with daylight.

[10] Empedocles (84b), whom Plato is following, compares the eye to a horn lantern, and explains that the fire confined in the eyeball is so fine as to pass through tissues impervious to water.

But when the kindred fire (of daylight) has departed at nightfall, the visual ray is cut off; for issuing out to encounter what is unlike it, it is itself changed and put out, no longer coalescing with the neighboring air, since this contains no fire. Hence it sees no longer, and further induces sleep. For when the eyelids, the protection devised by the gods for vision, are closed, they confine the power of the fire inside, and this e disperses and smooths out the motions within, and then quietness ensues. If this quiet be profound, the sleep that comes on has few dreams; but when some stronger motions are left, they give rise to images answering in character and number to the motions and the regions in which they persist—images 46 which are copies made inside and remembered when we awake in the world outside.

## *Mirror images* (46a-c)

There will now be little difficulty in understanding all that concerns the formation of images in mirrors and any smooth reflecting surface. As a result of the combination of the two fires inside and outside, and again as a consequence of the formation, on each occasion, at the smooth surface, of a single fire which is in various ways changed in form, all such reflections necessarily occur, the fire belonging to the face (seen) b coalescing, on the smooth and bright surface, with the fire belonging to the visual ray. Left appears right because reverse parts of the visual current come into contact with reverse parts (of the light from the face seen), contrary to the usual rule of impact. On the contrary, right appears right and left left, when the visual light changes sides in the act of coalescing with the light with which it does coalesce; and this happens when the smooth surface of the mirror, being curved upwards c at either side, throws the right part of the visual current to the left, and the left to the right. The same curvature turned lengthwise to the face makes the whole appear upside down, throwing the lower part of the ray toward the top and the upper part toward the bottom.

*Accessory causes contrasted with the purpose of sight and hearing* (46c-47e)

Now all these things are among the accessory causes which the god uses as subservient in achieving the best result that is possible. But the great mass of mankind regard them, not as accessories, but as the sole causes of all things, producing effects by cooling or heating, compacting or rarefying, and all such processes. But such things are incapable of any plan or intelligence for any purpose. For we must declare that the only existing thing which properly possesses intelligence is soul, and this is an invisible thing, whereas fire, water and earth, and air are all visible bodies; and a lover of intelligence and knowledge must necessarily seek first for the causation that belongs to the intelligent nature, and only in the second place for that which belongs to things that are moved by others and of necessity set yet others in motion. We too, then, must proceed on this principle: we must speak of both kinds of cause, but distinguish causes that work with intelligence to produce what is good and desirable, from those which, being destitute of reason, produce their sundry effects at random and without order.

Enough, then, of the secondary causes that have contributed to give the eyes the power they now possess; we must next speak of their highest function for our benefit, for the sake of which the god has given them to us. Sight, then, in my judgment is the cause of the highest benefits to us in that no word of our present discourse about the universe could ever have been spoken had we never seen stars, Sun, and sky. But as it is, the sight of day and night, of months and the revolving years, of equinox and solstice, has caused the invention of number and bestowed on us the notion of time and the study of the nature of the world; whence we have derived all philosophy, than which no greater boon has ever come or shall come to mortal man as a gift from heaven. This, then, I call the greatest benefit of eyesight; why harp upon all those things of less importance, for which one who loves not wisdom, if he were deprived of the sight of them, might "lament with idle moan"? For our part, rather let us speak of eyesight as the cause of this benefit, for these ends: the god invented and gave us vision in order that we might observe the circuits of intelligence in the heaven and profit by them for the revolutions of our own thought, which are akin to them, though ours be troubled and they are unperturbed; and that, by learning to know them and acquiring the power to compute them rightly according to nature, we might reproduce the perfectly unerring revolutions of the god and reduce to settled order the wandering motions in ourselves.

Of sound and hearing once more the same account may be given: they are a gift from heaven for the same intent and purpose. For not only was speech appointed to this same intent, to which it contributes in the largest measure, but also all that part of Music that is serviceable with respect to the hearing of sound is given for the sake of harmony; and harmony, whose motions are akin to the revolutions of the soul within us, has been given by the Muses to him whose commerce with them is guided by intelligence, not for the sake of irrational pleasure (which is now thought to be its utility), but as an ally against the inward discord that has come into the revolution of the soul, to bring it into order and consonance with itself. Rhythm also was a succor bestowed upon us by the same hands to the same intent, because in the most part of us our condition is lacking in measure and poor in grace.

## II. WHAT COMES ABOUT OF NECESSITY

The distinction drawn in the last paragraph between subsidiary causes and rational purpose has provided the transition to the second part of the dialogue, which begins here. The opening sentence describes the contents of the first part as the works wrought by the craftsmanship of divine intelligence. We have traced, in the structure of the visible universe and of man, the manifestations of benevolent purpose; but we have been perpetually reminded that the work of the most ungrudging benevolence cannot be perfect; it can only be "as good as possible." The Demiurge has been operating all through under certain given conditions, which he did not originate and which set a limit to the goodness of his work. We have now to bring into account that "other principle" concerned in the production. It is introduced under the names of Necessity and the Errant Cause.

If we consider the plan of the whole discourse, we see that Plato, who has hitherto been looking at the world, as it were, from above, and following the procedure of intelligence as it introduces order into chaos, now shifts to the opposite pole and approaches the world from the dark abyss that confronted its maker. Step by step he analyzes those elements which were pictured at the outset as "taken over" by the Demiurge—"all that was visible, not at rest, but in discordant and unordered motion" (30a). These factors are gradually distinguished, until we reach the fundamental factor, Space. Space being given, Plato can then proceed to discover elements of rational design even in the "tumultuous welter of fire, air, water, and earth." The geometrical shapes of the primary bodies are constructed; and once they are formed into regular particles of determinate size and shape, the transformation of one into another, which had bulked so large in earlier physical systems, can be translated into terms of the disintegration and reformation of these solids. In some degree, the sensible qualities (or "powers") which act upon our sense organs can then be correlated with the peculiarities of geometrical shape; and so we shall come back once more, at the end of this second part, to the mechanism of sensation and perception—that point of contact between the knowing soul and the external world, to which the first part has brought us here.

### *Necessity. The Errant Cause* (47e-48e)

The opening paragraph is of fundamental importance for the understanding of the whole discourse. It describes the relations between Reason and Necessity, and how they co-operate to produce the visible world.

## NECESSITY. THE ERRANT CAUSE 47

Now our foregoing discourse, save for a few matters,[1] has set forth the works wrought by the craftsmanship of Reason; but we must now set beside them the things that come about of Necessity. For the generation of this universe was a mixed result of the combination of Necessity and Reason. Reason overruled Necessity by persuading her to guide the greatest part of the things that become toward what is best; in that way and on that principle this universe was fashioned in the beginning by the victory of reasonable persuasion over Necessity. If, then, we are really to tell how it came into being on this principle, we must bring in also the Errant Cause—in what manner its nature is to cause motion. So we must return upon our steps thus, and taking, in its turn, a second principle concerned in the origin of these same things, start once more upon our present theme from the beginning, as we did upon the theme of our earlier discourse.

We must, in fact, consider in itself the nature of fire and water, air and earth, before the generation of the Heaven, and their condition before the Heaven was. For to this day no one has explained their generation, but we speak as if men knew what fire and each of the others is, positing them as original principles, elements (as it were, letters) of the universe; whereas one who has ever so little intelligence should not rank them in this analogy even so low as syllables. On this occasion, however, our contribution is to be limited as follows. We are not now to speak of the "first principle" or "principles"—or whatever name men choose to employ—of all things, if only on account of the difficulty of explaining what we think by our present method of exposition. You, then, must not demand the explanation of me; nor could I persuade myself that I should be right in taking upon myself so great a task; but holding fast to what I said at the outset—the worth of a probable account—I will try to give an explanation of all these matters in detail, no less probable than another, but more so, starting from the beginning in the same manner

---

[1] Namely, the account of the physical processes of vision, which are only secondary causes, subservient to the true "reason" for the gift of sight.

as before. So now once again at the outset of our discourse let us call upon a protecting deity to grant us safe passage through a strange and unfamiliar exposition to the conclusion that probability dictates; and so let us begin once more.

## The Receptacle of Becoming (48e-49a)

Our new starting point in describing the universe must, however, be a fuller classification than we made before. We then distinguished two things; but now a third must be pointed out. For our earlier discourse the two were sufficient: one postulated as model, intelligible and always unchangingly real; second, a copy of this model, which becomes and is visible. A third we did not then distinguish, thinking that the two would suffice; but now, it seems, the argument compels us to attempt to bring to light and describe a form difficult and obscure. What nature must we, then, conceive it to possess and what part does it play? This, more than anything else: that it is the Receptacle—as it were, the nurse—of all Becoming.

## Fire, Air, etc., are names of qualities, not of substances (49a-50a)

True, however, as this statement is, it needs to be put in clearer language; and that is hard, in particular because to that end it is necessary to raise a previous difficulty about fire and the things that rank with fire. It is hard to say, with respect to any one of these, which we ought to call really water rather than fire, or indeed which we should call by any given name rather than by all the names together or by each severally, so as to use language in a sound and trustworthy way. How, then, and in what terms are we to speak of this matter, and what is the previous difficulty that may be reasonably stated?

In the first place, take the thing we now call water. This, when it is compacted, we see (as we imagine) becoming earth and stones, and this same thing, when it is dissolved and dispersed, becoming wind and air; air becoming fire by being inflamed; and, by a reverse process, fire, when condensed and extinguished, returning once more to the form of air, and air coming together again and condensing as mist and cloud; and from these, as they are yet more closely compacted, flowing water; and from water once more earth and stones: and thus, as it appears, they transmit in a cycle the process of passing into one another. Since, then, in this way no one of these things ever makes its appearance as the *same* thing, which of them can we steadfastly affirm to be *this*—whatever it may be—and not something else, without blushing for ourselves? It cannot be done; but by far the safest course is to speak of them in the following terms. Whenever we observe a thing perpetually changing—fire, for example—in every case we should speak of fire not as "this," but as "what is of such and such a quality," nor of water as "this," but always as "what is of such and such a quality"; nor must we speak of anything else as having some permanence, among all the things we indicate by the expressions "this" or "that," imagining we are pointing out some definite thing. For they slip away and do not wait to be described as "that" or "this" or by any phrase that exhibits them as having permanent being. We should not use these expressions of any of them, but "that which is of a certain quality and has the same sort of quality as it perpetually recurs in the cycle"—that is the description we should use in the case of each and all of them. In fact, we must give the name "fire" to that which is at all times [2] of such and such a quality; and so with anything else that is in process of becoming. Only in speaking of that *in* which all of them are always coming to be, making their appearance and again vanishing out of it, may we use the words "this" or "that"; we must not apply any of these words to that which is of some quality—hot or cold or any of the opposites—or to any combination of these opposites.

[2] There is *at all times* (διὰ παντός) a certain amount of stuff that is fiery. This quality is sufficiently "alike" (ὅμοιον) to be recognized and named, though it is not an enduring substance, and is perpetually varying.

## *The Receptacle compared to a mass of plastic material* (50a-c)

But I must do my best to explain this thing once more in still clearer terms.

Suppose a man had molded figures of all sorts out of gold,[3] and were unceasingly to remold each into all the rest: then, if you should point to one of them and ask what it was, much the safest answer in respect of truth would be to say "gold," and never to speak of a triangle or any of the other figures that were coming to be in it as things that have being, since they are changing even while one is asserting their existence. Rather one should be content if they so much as consent to accept the description "what is of such and such a quality" with any certainty. Now the same thing must be said of that nature which receives all bodies. It must be called always the same; for it never departs at all from its own character; since it is always receiving all things, and never in any way whatsoever takes on any character that is like any of the things that enter it: by nature it is there as a matrix for everything, changed and diversified by the things that enter it, and on their account it *appears* to have different qualities at different times; while the things that pass in and out are to be called copies of the eternal things, impressions taken from them in a strange manner that is hard to express: we will follow it up on another occasion.[4]

## *The Receptacle has no qualities of its own* (50c-51b)

Be that as it may, for the present we must conceive three things: that which becomes; that in which it becomes; and the

---

[3] ἐκ χρυσοῦ. The figures are made *out of* gold and *consist of* gold; but the contents of the Receptacle are not made *out of* it. This is a point where the illustration is inadequate.

[4] The reference may be to 52c (A.-H.), or the promise may be unfulfilled (Tr.).

model in whose likeness that which becomes is born. Indeed we may fittingly compare the Recipient to a mother, the model to a father, and the nature that arises between them to their offspring. Further we must observe that, if there is to be an impress presenting all diversities of aspect, the thing itself in which the impress comes to be situated, cannot have been duly prepared unless it is free from all those characters which it is to receive from elsewhere. For if it were like any one of the things that come in upon it, then, when things of contrary or entirely different nature came, in receiving them it would reproduce them badly, intruding its own features alongside. Hence that which is to receive in itself all kinds must be free from all characters; just like the base which the makers of scented ointments skillfully contrive to start with: they make the liquids that are to receive the scents as odorless as possible. Or again, anyone who sets about taking impressions of shapes in some soft substance allows no shape to show itself there beforehand, but begins by making the surface as smooth and level as he can. In the same way, that which is duly to receive over its whole extent and many times over all the likenesses of the intelligible and eternal things ought in its own nature to be free of all the characters. For this reason, then, the mother and Receptacle of what has come to be visible and otherwise sensible must not be called earth or air or fire or water, nor any of their compounds or components;[5] but we shall not be deceived if we call it a nature invisible

---

[5] "Compounds," *i.e.*, complex bodies formed of more than one of the four primary bodies. "Components," *i.e.*, any qualities into which what we call "fire" or "fieriness" (etc.) might be analyzed, e.g. the heat, yellowness, etc., of flame. Cf. 50a, ὅσα ἐκ τούτων, where τούτων means the opposites (hot, white, etc.), of which fire, etc., are composed. This statement formally excludes the notion that the Receptacle is some subtler or more ultimate kind of matter (such as "the hot," "the cold," etc.) beyond the four primary bodies (cf. Fraccaroli, p. 89). At *Sophist* 243 the view that "the hot and the cold" are the ultimately real things in nature is taken as typical of all the early physicists. There is no reference to the triangles of which the elementary figures are later to be composed, since these have not yet been mentioned.

and characterless, all-receiving, partaking in some very puzzling way of the intelligible and very hard to apprehend. So far as its nature can be arrived at from what has already been said, the most correct account of it would be this: that part of it which has been made fiery appears at any time as fire; the part that is liquefied as water; and as earth or air such parts as receive likenesses of these.

### Ideal models of Fire, Air, Water, Earth (51b-e)

But in pressing our inquiry about them, there is a question that must rather be determined by argument. Is there such a thing as "Fire just in itself" or any of the other things which we are always describing in such terms, as things that "are just in themselves"? Or are the things we see or otherwise perceive by the bodily senses the only things that have such reality, and has nothing else, over and above these, any sort of being at all? Are we talking idly whenever we say that there is such a thing as an intelligible Form of anything? Is this nothing more than a word?

Now it does not become us either to dismiss the present question without trial or verdict, simply asseverating that it is so, nor yet to insert a lengthy digression into a discourse that is already long. If we could see our way to draw a distinction of great importance in few words, that would best suit the occasion. My own verdict, then, is this. If intelligence and true belief are two different kinds, then these things—Forms that we cannot perceive but only think of—certainly exist in themselves; but if, as some hold, true belief in no way differs from intelligence, then all the things we perceive through the bodily senses must be taken as the most certain reality. Now we must affirm that they are two different things, for they are distinct in origin and unlike in nature. The one is produced in us by instruction, the other by persuasion; the one can always give a true account of itself, the other can give none; the one cannot be shaken by persuasion, whereas the other can be won over; and true belief, we must allow, is shared by all mankind, intelligence only by the gods and a small number of men.

*Summary description of the three factors: Form, Copy, and Space as the Receptacle* (51e-52d)

This being so, we must agree that there is, first, the unchanging Form, ungenerated and indestructible, which neither receives anything else into itself from elsewhere nor itself enters into anything else anywhere, invisible and otherwise imperceptible; that, in fact, which thinking has for its object.

Second is that which bears the same name and is like that Form; is sensible; is brought into existence; is perpetually in motion, coming to be in a certain place and again vanishing out of it; and is to be apprehended by belief involving perception.

Third is Space, which is everlasting, not admitting destruction; providing a situation for all things that come into being, but itself apprehended without the senses by a sort of bastard reasoning, and hardly an object of belief.

This, indeed, is that which we look upon as in a dream and say that anything that is must needs be in some place and occupy some room, and that what is not somewhere in earth or heaven is nothing. Because of this dreaming state, we prove unable to rouse ourselves and to draw all these distinctions and others akin to them, even in the case of the waking and truly existing nature, and so to state the truth: namely that, whereas for an image, since not even the very principle on which it has come into being belongs to the image itself,[6] but it is the ever moving semblance of something else, it is proper that it should come to be *in* something else, clinging in some sort to existence on pain of being nothing at all, on the other hand that which has real being has the support of the exactly true account, which declares that, so long as the two things are

---

[6] An image comes into being on the same principle or conditions as a reflection: there must be an original to cast it and a medium to contain it. Neither condition "belongs to" the image itself.

different, neither can ever come to be in the other in such a way that the two should become at once one and the same thing and two.

## Description of Chaos (52d-53c)

Let this, then, be given as the tale summed according to my judgment: that there are Being, Space, Becoming—three distinct things—even before the Heaven came into being. Now the nurse of Becoming, being made watery and fiery and receiving the characters of earth and air, and qualified by all the other affections that go with these, had every sort of diverse appearance to the sight; but because it was filled with powers that were neither alike nor evenly balanced, there was no equipoise in any region of it; but it was everywhere swayed unevenly and shaken by these things, and by its motion shook them in turn. And they, being thus moved, were perpetually being separated and carried in different directions; just as when things are shaken and winnowed by means of winnowing baskets and other instruments for cleaning corn, the dense and heavy things go one way, while the rare and light are carried to another place and settle there. In the same way at that time the four kinds were shaken by the Recipient, which itself was in motion like an instrument for shaking, and it separated the most unlike kinds farthest apart from one another, and thrust the most alike closest together; whereby the different kinds came to have different regions, even before the ordered whole consisting of them came to be. Before that, all these kinds were without proportion or measure. Fire, water, earth, and air possessed indeed some vestiges of their own nature, but were altogether in such a condition as we should expect for anything when deity is absent from it. Such being their nature at the time when the ordering of the universe was taken in hand, the god then began by giving them a distinct configuration by means of shapes and numbers. That the god framed them with the greatest possible perfection, which they had not before, must be taken, above all, as a principle we constantly assert; what I must now attempt to explain to you is the distinct formation of each and their origin. The account will be unfamiliar; but you are schooled in those branches of learning which my explanations require, and so will follow me.

### Construction of the figures of the four primary bodies
### (53c-55c)

In the first place, then, it is of course obvious to anyone that fire, earth, water, and air are bodies; and all body has depth. Depth, moreover, must be bounded by surface;[7] and every surface that is rectilinear is composed of triangles. Now all triangles are derived from two, each having one right angle and the other angles acute. Of these triangles, one has on either side the half of a right angle, the division of which is determined by equal sides (the right-angled isosceles); the other has unequal parts of a right angle allotted to unequal sides (the right-angled scalene). This we assume as the first beginning of fire and of the other bodies, following the account which combines likelihood with necessity;[8] the principles yet more remote than these are known to Heaven and to such men as Heaven favors.

Now, the question to be determined is this: What are the most perfect bodies that can be constructed, four in number, unlike one another, but such that some can be generated out of one another by resolution? If we can hit upon the answer to this, we have the truth concerning the generation of earth and fire and of the bodies which stand as proportionals between them. For we shall concede to no one that there are visible bodies more perfect than these, each corresponding

---

[7] "Surface," not "plane," since some solids have curved surfaces.

[8] The account is "likely" because we cannot know that the whole theory which assigns the figures of regular solids to the primary bodies is the truth. It is combined with "necessity" in that the necessarily given properties of Space and the logical necessity of geometrical construction are involved in the consequence of the initial assumption.

to a single type.⁹ We must do our best, then, to construct the four types of body that are most perfect and declare that we have grasped the constitution of these things sufficiently for our purpose.¹⁰

Now, of the two triangles, the isosceles is of one type only; the scalene, of an endless number. Of this unlimited multitude we must choose the best, if we are to make a beginning on our own principles. Accordingly, if anyone can tell us of a better kind that he has chosen for the construction of these bodies, his will be the victory, not of an enemy, but of a friend. For ourselves, however, we postulate as the best of these many triangles one kind, passing over all the rest; that, namely, a pair of which compose the equilateral triangle. The reason is too long a story; but if anyone should put the matter to the test and discover that it is not so, the prize is his with all good will. So much, then, for the choice of the two triangles, of which the bodies of fire and of the rest have been wrought: the one isosceles (the half-square), the other having the greater side triple in square of the lesser (the half-equilateral).

We must now be more precise upon a point that was not clearly enough stated earlier.¹¹ It appeared as though all the four kinds could pass through one another into one another; but this appearance is delusive; for the triangles we selected give rise to four types, and whereas three are constructed out of the triangle with unequal sides, the fourth alone is constructed out of the isosceles. Hence it is not possible for all of them to pass into one another by resolution, many of the small forming a few of the greater and vice versa. But three of them can do this; for these are all composed of one triangle,

---

⁹ "Type" (γένος) here seems to mean "type of solid figure," as in the next sentence.

¹⁰ ἱκανῶς: "sufficiently" in order to explain the physical transformation of the primary bodies ("these things"), whereas the full geometrical construction would be a much longer business.

¹¹ At 53e it was said that *some* (but not all) primary bodies could pass into one another by resolution. The next sentence refers to 49b, c.

# FIGURES OF THE PRIMARY BODIES

and when the larger bodies are broken up, several small ones will be formed of the same triangles, taking on their proper figures; and again when several of the smaller bodies are dispersed into their triangles, the total number made up by them will produce a single new figure of larger size, belonging to a single body. So much for their passing into one another.[12]

The next thing to explain is, what sort of figure each body has, and the numbers [13] that combine to compose it.

First will come the construction of the simplest and smallest figure (the pyramid). Its element is the triangle whose hypotenuse is double of the shorter side in length. If a pair of such triangles are put together by the diagonal,[14] and this is

d

[12] The exclusion of earth from the cycle of transformation is simply a consequence of the decision to assign the cube to earth. Other physicists (including Aristotle) felt no objection to earth being transformed; and the exclusion is certainly not dictated by any facts of observation, to which, indeed, Plato makes no appeal. Plato now proceeds to build the four regular solids. He begins with the construction of the equilateral triangular face which is common to the pyramid, the octahedron, and the icosahedron. The "element" is the half-equilateral, "whose hypotenuse is double of the shorter side in length." The equilateral is formed by putting together six (not, as we should expect, two) of these elements in the following figure:

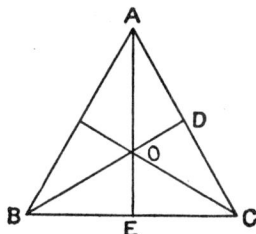

[13] "Numbers" may mean "numbers of units," i.e. elementary triangles; but there are also the numbers of faces, angles, etc., in the solid.

[14] Probably, the diagonal of the resulting figure, the trapezium *CDOE*, viz., the hypotenuse *CO*. Since there is no question of proper geometrical methods of construction, but only of fitting pieces together as in a puzzle, there is no objection to building an equilateral out of trapezia. Not using diagrams, Plato simply describes the figure as briefly as he can.

## 58 FIGURES OF THE PRIMARY BODIES

e done three times, the diagonals and the shorter sides resting on the same point as a center, in this way a single equilateral triangle is formed of triangles six in number. If four equilateral triangles are put together, their plane angles meeting in groups of three make a single solid angle, namely the one
55 (180°) that comes next after the most obtuse of plane angles. When four such angles are produced, the simplest solid figure is formed, whose property is to divide the whole circumference into equal and similar parts.

A second body (the octahedron) is composed of the same (elementary) triangles when they are combined in a set of eight equilateral triangles, and yield a solid angle formed by four plane angles. With the production of six such solid angles the second body is complete.

The third body (the icosahedron) is composed of one hundred and twenty of the elementary triangles fitted together,
b and of twelve solid angles, each contained by five equilateral triangular planes; and it has twenty faces which are equilateral triangles.

Here one of the two elements, having generated these bodies, had done its part. But the isosceles triangle went on to generate the fourth body, being put together in sets of four, with their right angles meeting at the center, thus forming a single equilateral quadrangle.[15]

c Six such quadrangles, joined together, produced eight solid

---

[15] The second elementary triangle, the half-square, is now used to construct the square face of the cube. Here again Plato uses more elements than are necessary—four instead of two. This is another point which we will hold in reserve.

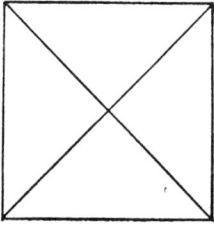

angles, each composed by a set of three plane right angles. The shape of the resulting body was cubical, having six quadrangular equilateral planes as its faces.

There still remained one construction, the fifth; and the god used it for the whole, making a pattern of animal figures thereon.[16]

## Might there be five worlds? (55c-d)

Now if anyone, taking all these things into account, should raise the pertinent question, whether the number of worlds should be called indefinite or limited, he would judge that  d to call them indefinite is the opinion of one who is indeed indefinite about matters on which he ought to be definitely informed. But whether it is proper to speak of them as being really one or five, he might, if he stopped short there, more reasonably feel a doubt. Our own verdict, indeed, declares the world to be by nature a single god, according to the probable account; but another, looking to other considerations, will judge differently. He, however, may be dismissed.

[16] [This is the dodecahedron. It] is not constructed. Plato knew that its pentagonal faces cannot be formed out of either of his two elementary triangles: it was in fact constructed by means of an isosceles triangle having each of its base angles double of the vertical angle. Not requiring a dodecahedron with plane faces for any primary body, the Demiurge "uses it for the whole," i.e., for the sphere, to which this figure approaches most nearly in volume, as Timaeus Locrus remarks. The meaning is explained in Wyttenbach's note on *Phaedo* 110b, where Socrates says that the spherical Earth, seen from above, would resemble "one of those balls made of twelve pieces of leather" marked out in a pattern of various colors. "To make a ball, we take twelve pieces of leather, each of which is a regular pentagon. If the material were not flexible, we should have a regular dodecahedron; as it is flexible, we get a ball." So here Plato imagines a flexible dodecahedron expanding into spherical shape. The word $\delta\iota\alpha\zeta\omega\gamma\rho\alpha\phi\tilde{\omega}\nu$ is ambiguous. It might mean "giving it a pattern of various colors"; but this seems hardly appropriate to the sky. On the other hand, the whole sky is covered with "animals"—not only the twelve signs of the Zodiac, but all the other constellations.

### Assignment of the regular figures to the four primary bodies (55d-56c)

Let us next distribute the figures whose formation we have now described, among fire, earth, water, and air.

To earth let us assign the cubical figure; for of the four kinds earth is the most immobile and the most plastic of bodies.[17] The figure whose bases are the most stable must best answer that description; and as a base, if we take the triangles we assumed at the outset, the face of the triangle with equal sides is by nature more stable than that of the triangle whose sides are unequal; and further, of the two equilateral surfaces respectively composed of the two triangles, the square is necessarily a more stable base than the triangle, both in its parts and as a whole. Accordingly we shall preserve the probability of our account, if we assign this figure to earth; and of the remainder the least mobile to water, the most mobile to fire, and the intermediate figure to air. Again, we shall assign the smallest[18] body to fire, the largest to water, and the intermediate to air; and again the body with the sharpest angles to fire, the next to air, the third to water.

Now, taking all these figures, the one with the fewest faces (pyramid) must be the most mobile, since it has the sharpest cutting edges and the sharpest points in every direction, and

---

[17] "Plastic," as retaining any shape into which it is moulded. "Immobile" is equivalent to "hard to move" (δυσκίνητος below; "unyielding," "sluggish" A.-H.), not "stable," for the icosahedron (water) is said to be the hardest to move of the other three bodies, whereas it is the least stable of them (a fact noted at 58d). In a mixed mass of solids of all the types the cubes would be the hardest to shift, the pyramids the easiest because their edges and points are sharp, so that a slighter thrust would push them between the rest. The next sentence argues that earth is hardest to shift and most plastic because it is also the most stable.

[18] As Tr. remarks (p. 381), we shall hear later that there are several grades of size for each primary body, but that point is left out of account until it is actually mentioned at 57c. It is here assumed that all three bodies have equilateral faces of the same size.

moreover the lightest, as being composed of the smallest number of similar parts;[19] the second (octahedron) must stand second in these respects, the third (icosahedron), third. Hence, in accordance with genuine reasoning as well as probability, among the solid figures we have constructed, we may take the pyramid as the element or seed of fire;[20] the second in order of generation (octahedron) as that of air; the third (icosahedron) as that of water.

Now we must think of all these bodies[21] as so small that a single body of any one of these kinds is invisible to us because of its smallness; though when a number are aggregated the masses of them can be seen. And with regard to their numbers, their motions, and their powers in general, we must suppose that the god adjusted them in due proportion, when he had brought them in every detail to the most exact perfection permitted by Necessity willingly complying with persuasion.

## *Transformation of the primary bodies* (56c-57c)

Now, from all that we have said in the foregoing account concerning the kinds, the following would be the most probable description of the facts.

---

[19] Cf. 58e, Water composed of large particles is harder to move and *heavy;* 59c, Bronze is *lighter* than gold because it has larger interstices. According to the analysis of lightness and heaviness at 62c ff., a larger quantity of any primary body is heavier than a smaller one, and this only means that it offers a greater resistance to the attempt to force it away from its proper region. Since it will be forced into the region of another element and have to make its way through that, the "nimblest" body will also be the "lightest." It will be easier to force a fire pyramid in among the octahedra of air than to force an octahedron in among the pyramids.

[20] "Element" because, when the pyramid is broken up into the elements proper (the triangles), fire ceases to exist as such, with the "motions and powers" characteristic of it (though on this point Plato is not quite clear later). "Seed" (a term applied to the microscopic bodies in Anaxagoras' system) is added to show that "element" has this sense here.

[21] All the four, to which these concluding remarks apply (not, as Tr. says, p. 382, the three last named only).

Earth, when it meets with fire and is dissolved by its sharpness, would drift about—whether, when dissolved, it be enveloped in fire itself or in a mass of air or of water—until its own parts somewhere encounter one another, are fitted together, and again become earth; for they can never pass into any other kind.

But (1) when water is divided into parts by fire, or again by air, it is possible for one particle of fire and two of air to arise by combination; and (2) the fragments of air, from a single particle that is dissolved, can become two particles of fire. And conversely, (3) when a little fire, enveloped in a large quantity of air or water or (it may be) earth, is kept in motion within these masses which are moving in place, and makes a fight, and then is overcome and shattered into fragments, two particles of fire combine to make a single figure of air. And (4) when air is overpowered and broken small, from two and a half complete figures, a single complete figure of water will be compacted.

Let us reconsider this account once more as follows. (*a*) When one of the other kinds is enveloped in fire and cut up by the sharpness of its angles and edges, then (α), if it is recombined into the shape of fire, there is an end to the cutting up; for no kind which is homogeneous and identical can effect any change in, or suffer any change from, that which is in the same condition as itself. But (β) so long as, passing into some other kind, a weaker body is contending with a stronger, the resolution does not come to an end.

And, on the other hand, (*b*) when a few smaller particles are enveloped in a large number of bigger ones and are being shattered and quenched,[22] then, (α) if they consent to combine into the figure of the prevailing kind, the quenching process comes to an end: from fire comes air, from air, water. But (β) if they (the smaller particles) are on their way to these (air or water), and one of the other kinds meets them and comes into

[22] "Quenched" shows that Plato is thinking in particular of fire enveloped in larger particles (as at 56e); but the statement applies also to air passing straight into water, as the last words of the sentence show.

conflict, the process of their resolution does not stop until either they are wholly dissolved by the thrusting and escape to their kindred, or they are overcome and a number of them form a single body uniform with the victorious body and take up their abode with it.

Moreover, in the course of suffering this treatment, they are c all interchanging their regions. For while the main masses of the several kinds are stationed apart, each in its own place, owing to the motion of the Recipient, the portions which at any time are becoming unlike themselves and like other kinds are borne by the shaking toward the place of those others to which they become like.

### Each primary body exists in various grades of size (57c-d)

In this way, then, the formation of all the uncompounded and primary bodies is accounted for. The reason why there are several varieties within their kinds lies in the construction of each of the two elements: the construction in each case originally produced its triangle not of one size only, but some d smaller, some larger, the number of these differences being the same as that of the varieties in the kinds. Hence, when they are mixed with themselves or with one another, there is an endless diversity, which must be studied by one who is to put forward a probable account of Nature.

### Motion and Rest (57d-58c)

Now concerning motion and rest, if we do not agree in what manner and in what conditions they arise, many difficulties will stand in the way of our subsequent reasoning. Something e has already been said about them, but there is this to be added: motion will never exist in a state of homogeneity. For it is difficult, or rather impossible, that what is to be moved should exist without that which is to move it, or what is to cause motion without that which is to be moved by it. In the absence of either, motion cannot exist; and they cannot possibly be homogeneous. Accordingly, we must always presume rest in a state of homogeneity, and attribute motion to a condition that is heterogeneous. Further, inequality is a cause of heterogeneity; and the origin of inequality we have already described.[23]

But we have not explained how it is that the several bodies have not been completely separated apart in their kinds and so ceased to pass through one another and to change their place. We must, then, resume our explanation as follows. The circuit of the whole, when once it has comprehended the (four) kinds, being round and naturally tending to come together upon itself, constricts them all and allows (*or* tends to allow) no room to be left empty. Hence fire has, more than all the rest, penetrated in among all the others;[24] and, in the second degree, air, as being second in the fineness of its particles; and so on with the rest. For the kinds that are composed of the largest particles leave the largest gaps in their texture, while the smallest bodies leave the least.[25] So the coming together involved in the condensing process thrusts the small bodies together into the interstices between the large ones. Accordingly, when the small are set alongside the large, and the lesser disintegrate[26] the larger, while the larger cause the lesser to combine, all are changing the direction of their

---

[23] Obviously the mover here cannot be the soul, which belongs to a higher order of existence. It could not be spoken of as either heterogeneous and unequal, or homogeneous and equal, with the moved.

[24] Cf. 78a: "Of all the kinds fire has the smallest particles and consequently passes through ($\delta\iota\alpha\chi\omega\rho\epsilon\hat{\iota}$) water, earth, and air and all bodies composed of these, and nothing is impervious to it."

[25] The icosahedra composing a mass of water, however closely packed, must, owing to their shape, leave larger gaps between them than those left between the octahedra (of the same grade) in a mass of air.

[26] $\delta\iota\alpha\kappa\rho\iota\nu\acute{o}\nu\tau\omega\nu$. If the particles were atoms, $\delta\iota\alpha\kappa\rho\acute{\iota}\nu\epsilon\iota\nu$ could only mean "separate" and $\sigma\upsilon\gamma\kappa\rho\acute{\iota}\nu\epsilon\iota\nu$ "bring together"; but since particles can be broken up into elementary triangles, the breaking down and recombining of these elements may be meant; and the reference to change of figure seems to imply this. As we have seen (56d), disintegration is chiefly caused by the smallest body, fire. At 56e we learned how the larger bodies (air and water) cause fragments of the lesser to recombine in the larger figures.

movement, this way and that, toward their own regions; for each, in changing its size, changes also the situation of its region. In this way, then, and by these means there is a perpetual safeguard for the occurrence of that heterogeneity which provides that the perpetual motion of these bodies is and shall be without cessation.

### Varieties and compounds of the primary bodies (58c-61c)

Next we must observe that there are several varieties of fire: flame; that effluence from flame which does not burn but gives light to the eyes; and what is left of fire in glowing embers when flame is quenched. And so with air: there is the brightest and clearest kind called "ether," and the most turbid called "murk" and "gloom," and other nameless kinds, whose formation is accounted for by the inequality of the triangles.

### Water, liquid and fusible: melting and cooling of the fusible

Of water, the primary division is into two types: (1) the liquid, and (2) the fusible.

(1) The liquid, because it contains portions of the small grades of water, unequal in size, is in itself mobile and can be readily set in motion by something else, owing to its non-uniformity and the shape of its figure.

(2) The other (fusible) type composed of large and uniform particles is harder to move than the former and heavy, being set hard by its uniformity. But under the action of fire, making its way in and breaking it down, it loses its uniformity, and consequently becomes more mobile; and when it has become quite easy to move, under the thrust of the neighboring air it is spread over the ground. Each of these two processes has received a name: "melting" for the reduction in bulk of the particles, "flowing" for the spreading over the ground.

When, on the contrary, the fire is being expelled from it again, since the fire does not pass out into vacancy, the neighboring air receives a thrust and itself thrusts together the liquid mass, while it is still quite easily moved, into the places left by the fire and makes it a homogeneous combination. The liquid, being so thrust together and regaining its uniformity, as the fire which created the lack of uniformity departs, settles into its original state. The departure of the fire is called "cooling"; the contraction that follows on its withdrawal is referred to as "being in a solid state."

*Some varieties of the fusible type (metals): gold, adamant, copper*

Of all these fusible varieties of water, as we have called them, one that is very dense, being formed of very fine and uniform particles, unique in its kind, tinged with shining and yellow hue, is gold, the treasure most highly prized, which has been filtered through rock and there compacted.

The "scion of gold," which is very hard because of its density and is darkly colored, is called adamant.

Another has particles nearly like those of gold, but of more than one grade; in point of density in one way it surpasses gold and it is harder because it contains a small portion of fine earth; but it is lighter by reason of containing large interstices. This formation is copper, one of the bright and solid kinds of water. The portion of earth mixed with it appears by itself on the surface when the two substances begin to be separated again by the action of time; it is called verdigris.

It would be no intricate task to enumerate the other substances of this kind, following the method of a probable account. When a man, for the sake of recreation, lays aside discourse about eternal things and gains an innocent pleasure from the consideration of such plausible accounts of becoming, he will add to his life a sober and sensible pastime. So now we will give it rein and go on to set forth the probabilities that come next in this subject as follows.

*Solidification of fluids: Water, hail, ice, snow, hoar-frost*

Water that is mixed with fire and is fine and liquid (it is called "liquid" because of its motion and its rolling course

JUICES 67

over the ground), and also soft because its bases give way, being less stable than those of earth—water of this sort, when it is separated off from fire and air and left by itself, becomes more uniform, and at the same time is thrust together upon itself by the action of the particles that are passing out of it.[27] e Water so compacted, when it suffers this change to the extreme degree above the earth, is hail; when on the ground, ice. Water that is less affected and still only half congealed is called "snow" above the earth, and when congealed from dew on the ground is known as "hoarfrost."

*Some varieties of the liquid type (juices)*

Mixtures composed of most of the grades of water are given the general name of juices, being filtered through the plants 60 that grow out of the earth; while their several differences are due to the variety of combinations. A great number of the varieties they present are nameless; but the four kinds which contain fire are specially conspicuous and have received names. One is wine, which heats soul and body together; next, the oily kind, which is smooth and divides the visual current and therefore appears bright and shining to the view and glistens: [28] resin, castor oil, olive oil itself, and all the rest that have the same property; third, the kind that relaxes the contracted pores in the region of the mouth to their normal b condition,[29] producing sweetness by this property, has received the general name of honey; [30] last, a kind that dissolves the

[27] The particles do not pass out into vacancy but (as before, 59a) expand the surrounding air, which thus exerts pressure on the liquid.
[28] Cf. 67e.
[29] The correct explanation is due to A.-H. So Tr. The property (δύναμις) resides in the object as its power of acting on the sense organ. Sweetness is a quality of the honey produced by commerce with the sentient organ and existing only while sensation is taking place (*Theaet.* 159d). Sweetness as a quality of the sensation experienced is described at 66c, and attributed to the same causes.
[30] The "honey" found in flowers, rather than the stuff made by bees. The word also covers sweet gums exuded by certain trees, e.g., ἐλαιόμελι.

flesh by burning, a frothy substance distinct (?) from all the other juices, which is called "acrid juice." [81]

*Varieties and compounds of earth: stone and earthenware; soda and salt; glass and wax*

Of the varieties of earth, that which has been strained through water becomes a stony substance in the following way. When the water mixed with it is broken up in the mixing, it changes into the form of air; [32] and when it has become air, it rushes up toward its own region. But there was no empty space surrounding it; accordingly it gives a thrust to the neighboring air. This air, being heavy,[33] when it is thrust and poured round the mass of earth, squeezes it hard and thrusts it together into the places from which the new-made air has been rising. Earth thrust together by air so as not to be soluble by water forms stone, the finer being the transparent kind consisting of equal and homogeneous particles, the baser of the opposite sort.

The kind that has been robbed of all moisture by the rapid action of fire, a formation more brittle than the other, is what we have named "earthenware"; but sometimes, when some moisture is left and the result is earth that is fusible by fire, the dark-colored stuff produced when it cools is lava (?).

---

[31] ἐκ πάντων ἀφορισθὲν τῶν χυμῶν, ὀπὸς ἐπωνομάσθη. The meaning of ὀπός here is doubtful. Galen says that there are a very great number of ὀποί, since the word means the thick and sticky stuff that flows from an incision in any root or stalk; but it is more specifically used of silphium juice (ὀπὸς κυρηναικός). Theophrastus uses ὀπός for plant juice, and specially for silphium and for fig juice, used in curdling milk. In our passage it obviously means bitter juice, and is probably (like μέλι) the general name for a whole class.

[32] Here the transformation of one body into another is involved, as we suggested might be the case in the solidification of water (59e).

[33] Heavy in the popular sense, since it exerts a downward pressure (as well as in other directions) which reacts on the earth, as at 59a. This has no connection with the natural drift of every body to its proper region.

There are, again, two kinds which are left in the same way when a great amount of water has departed from the mixture; but the particles of earth in their composition are finer and they have a saline taste. These become only half solid and are soluble again by water. The one, which cleanses from grease and dirt, is soda; the other product, which blends agreeably in the combinations of flavor, is salt, a substance which, according to human convention, is pleasing to heaven.

The compounds of both (earth and water) which are soluble by fire, but not by water, are compacted in that manner for the following reason:

(1) Masses of earth are not dissolved by fire or air, because their particles are smaller than the interstices in the texture of earth, so that, having plenty of room to pass through without forcing their way, they do not loosen the earth but leave it undissolved; whereas the particles of water, being larger, make their passage through by force and so loosen the earth and dissolve it. Earth, then, is dissolved in this way by water only, when it is not forcibly compressed; but if it is so compressed only fire can dissolve it, for no entrance is left for anything but fire. (2) Water, again, when most forcibly compressed is dispersed by fire only; though when the consistency is weaker, both fire and air disperse it, air by its interstices, fire actually breaking it down into its triangles; while (3) air forcibly compressed cannot be resolved by anything save into its elements, and when not so compressed, is dissolved only by fire.

So in these bodies compounded of earth and water, so long as water occupies the interstices of the earth in such a body, though these may be forcibly compressed, the particles of water assailing it from outside can find no entrance, so that, flowing round the whole mass, they leave it undissolved; whereas the particles of fire make their way into the interstices between the water particles and, acting upon them—fire upon water—in the same way that water acts upon earth, are the only agents that can cause the compound body to be dissolved and set flowing. Of these compounds, some contain less water than earth, namely all kinds of glass and any varieties of stone that are called fusible; others contain more water, namely, all the substances with a consistency like that of wax or incense.

### Tactile qualities, as they appear to sensation and perception (61c-64a)

We have now, perhaps, sufficiently illustrated the varieties due to diversity of shapes, combinations, and transformations of one body into another. Next we must try to make clear how it is that they come to have their qualities.

First, then, our account at every point must assume the existence of sensation; but we have not yet described the formation of flesh and all that belongs to flesh, or the mortal part of soul.[34] Yet no adequate account can be given of these apart from all those qualities that are connected with sensation, nor yet of the latter apart from the former; and to treat of both together is hardly possible. We must, then, first assume one side, and afterward turn back to examine what we have assumed. So, in order that our account may proceed from the kinds of body to their qualities, let us take for granted what is involved in the existence of body and soul.[35]

First, then, let us see how it is that we call fire "hot." We may study this question by observing the rending and cutting effect of fire upon our bodies. We are all aware that the sensation is a piercing one; and we may infer the fineness of the edges, the sharpness of the angles, the smallness of the particles, and the swiftness of the movement, all of which properties make fire energetic and trenchant, cleaving and piercing whatever it encounters. When we recall the formation of its

---

[34] It has been stated (42a) that the implanting of the immortal part in a body entails, of necessity, the faculty of "sensation ($αἴσθησις$) arising from violent impressions," pleasure and pain, desire and passion. But the only senses so far dealt with in any detail were sight and hearing (45b ff.), not touch, and nothing has yet been said about the differences of quality as perceived in colors and sounds.

[35] The mortal parts of the soul and the main bodily organs are reserved for the third part of the discourse, from 69a onward.

## TACTILE QUALITIES

figure we see that this substance, more than any other, penetrates the body and divides it minutely and naturally gives the affection we call "hot" its quality and its name.

The opposite quality is obvious enough, but it shall not go without an explanation. The particles of fluids in the neighborhood of the body, when they enter it, thrust out the particles smaller than themselves,[36] and not being able to insert themselves into their places they compress the moisture in us and solidify it by reducing what was not uniform and was therefore in motion to immobility, resulting from uniformity and compression. But a thing that is unnaturally contracted struggles, pushing itself apart again into its normal state. This struggling and shaking is called trembling and shivering; and the name "cold" is given to this affection as a whole and to the agent producing it.

"Hard" is applied to anything to which our flesh yields, "soft," to anything that yields to flesh; and hard and soft things are also so called with reference to one another. A thing is yielding when it has a small base; the figure composed of square faces, having a firm standing, is most stubborn; so too is anything that is specially resistant because it is contracted to the greatest density.

"Heavy" and "light" may be most clearly explained by examining them together with the expressions "above" and "below." It is entirely wrong to suppose that there are by nature two opposite regions dividing the universe between them, one "below," toward which all things sink that have bodily bulk, the other "above," toward which everything is reluctant to rise. For since the whole heaven is spherical in shape, all the points which are extreme in virtue of being equally distant from the center must be extremities in just the

[36] I take these smaller particles to be fire and air (not a smaller grade of water particles). Cf. the descriptions of cooling by loss of fire particles (59a), and of freezing by isolation of water particles from fire and air and consequent increase of uniformity (59d, e). There seems to be no reason why larger water particles from outside should expel smaller water particles already present in the body; and we do not in fact sweat when we are getting cold. The moisture in us is not expelled but compressed.

same manner; while the center, being distant by the same measure from all the extremes, must be regarded as at the point "opposite" to them all. Such being the nature of the ordered world, which of the points mentioned could one call either "above" or "below" without being justly censured for using a quite unsuitable term? The central region in it does not deserve to be described as being, in its nature, either above or below, but simply at the center; while the circumference is not, of course, central, nor is there any difference, distinguishing one part of it from another with reference to the center, which does not belong equally to some part on the opposite side.[37]

When a thing [38] is uniform in every direction, what pair of contrary terms can be applied to it and in what sense could they be properly used? If we further suppose that there is a solid body poised at the center of it all, this body will not move toward any of the points on the extremity, because in every direction they are all alike; rather, if a man were actually to walk round and round that body, he would repeatedly stand at his own antipodes and call the same point on its surface "above" and "below." [39] For the whole being spherical,

[37] This is the counterpart of the statement above, that the center cannot be called "above" the "lower" hemisphere or "below" the "upper" hemisphere. The next sentence asks to what these contrasted terms, above and below, can be applied, if neither the center nor any part of the circumference exhibits any corresponding difference of nature.

[38] This paragraph is in general terms, referring to *any* spherical figure, at the center of which is a solid body. It *applies* to the actual universe, because this has a solid body at its center, viz., the Earth.

[39] The connection between the two parts of this sentence becomes clear if we take the first part to mean that there is no reason why the central body should *fall down* in any direction, because there is no "down" for it to fall toward. On the contrary, the supposed traveler will be using "above" and "below" with reference to every direction in succession, since at any moment he will think he is "on the top" of the body which is "beneath him." Neither word, accordingly, stands for any inherent difference between the parts of the central body or of the universe as a whole. Paraphrasing this passage, Aristotle (*de caelo*, 308a, 20) assumes as

as we said just now, there is no sense in speaking of one region as above, another below.

As to the source of these terms and the things to which they really apply and which have occasioned our habit of using the words to describe a division of the universe as a whole, we may arrive at an agreement, if we make the following supposition. Imagine a man in that region of the universe which is specially allotted to fire, taking his stand on the main mass toward which fire moves, and suppose it possible for him to detach portions of fire and weigh them in the scales of a balance. When he lifts the beam and forcibly drags the fire into the alien air, clearly he will get the smaller portion to yield to force more readily than the greater; for when two masses at once are raised aloft by the same power, the lesser must follow the constraint more readily than the greater, which will make more resistance; and so the large mass will be said to be "heavy" and to tend "downward," the small to be "light" and to tend "upward." Now this is just what we ought to detect ourselves doing here in our own region. Standing on the Earth, when we are trying to distinguish between earthy substances or sometimes pure earth, we are dragging the two things into the alien air by violence and against their nature; both cling to their own kind, but the smaller yields more readily to our constraint than the larger and follows it more quickly into the alien element. Accordingly we have come to call it "light" and the region into which we force it "above"; when the thing behaves in the opposite way, we speak of "heavy" and "below." Consequently, the relation of these things to one another must vary, because the main masses of the kinds occupy regions opposite to one another: what is "light" or "heavy" or "above" or "below" in one region will all be found to become, or be, contrary to what is "light" or "heavy" or "above" or "below" in the opposite region, or to

---

a matter of course that the body round which the traveler walks is the earth, which actually occupies the center of Plato's world.

be inclined at an angle, with every possible difference of direction.[40] The one thing to be observed in all cases, however, is that it is the traveling of each kind toward its kindred that makes the moving thing "heavy" and the region to which it moves "below," while the contrary names are given to their opposites. So much for the explanation of these affections.

As for the qualities "smooth" and "rough," anyone, I suppose, could see how they are to be explained. Roughness is due to a combination of hardness and unevenness, smoothness to evenness combined with closeness of texture.

## *Pleasure and Pain* (64a-65b)

Concerning the affections common to the body as a whole, the most important point that remains to be considered is the explanation of the element of pleasantness or painfulness in those which we have just discussed; and further all those affections which, having attained to sensation through the organs of the body, may be also accompanied by inherent pains or pleasures.[41]

Now in seeking the explanation of any affection, whether perceptible or imperceptible, we must begin by recalling the distinction drawn earlier between what is mobile in structure and what is immobile; all the explanations we are bent upon discovering are to be sought along this line. When something that is naturally mobile is invaded by even a slight affection, it spreads it all round, one particle passing on the same effect to another, until they reach the consciousness and report the

---

[40] Thus, Earth being at the center and fire all around the circumference, so that "the main masses occupy opposite regions," the line along which a stone falls to earth or fire rises will be in a different direction for every point on the Earth's surface.

[41] In this sentence the first part refers to the "affections" above discussed, viz., qualities of objects as perceived, and what is meant by calling these pleasant or painful (capable of causing pleasure or pain to a sentient being). The second half refers to "affections" occurring within the body and transmitted through the organs to the soul, where they "acquire" sensation with (or without) pleasure or pain.

quality of the agent. The immobile, on the other hand, being too stable to spread the motion round, merely suffers the affection without setting any of its neighbors in motion; accordingly, since the particles do not pass it on one to another, the original affection remains in them incapable of transmission to the living creature as a whole and leaves the subject without sensation. This is the case with bone and hair and all the other parts in our bodies that are composed chiefly of earth; whereas the previously mentioned conditions apply to sight and hearing above all, because in them fire and air play the largest part.

The nature of pleasure and pain, then, must be conceived as follows. An affection which violently disturbs the normal state, if it happens all of a sudden, is painful, while the sudden restoration of the normal state is pleasant; these are perceptible, whereas a gentle and gradual change of either sort is imperceptible.

Any process, however, that takes place with great facility yields perceptions [42] in the highest degree, but it is not attended by pain or pleasure. Such are the affections that occur in the visual ray itself, which was, in fact, described earlier as a body formed in the daylight in intimate connection with our own. No pain is set up by cuts or burns in this ray or by anything else that is done to it, nor yet pleasure when it returns to its former condition, although there are intense and very distinct perceptions, according as it is acted upon and itself meets and touches any object; for no violence whatsoever is involved when the ray is severed and comes together again. On the other hand, organs consisting of larger particles, which yield to the agent reluctantly and pass on the motions to the whole, have pleasures and pains—pains while they are being ousted from their normal state, pleasures while this is being restored. Those in which the departure from the normal state or depletion is gradual, while the replenishment is sud-

---

[42] Literally "is perceptible," but the perception in the following instance of vision is perception of color, not of the disturbance, which yields no sensation at all, either pleasant or painful.

den and on a large scale, are sensible of the replenishment, but not of the depletion, and so afford to the mortal part of the soul [43] intense pleasures, but no pain. This is plain in the case of sweet smells. Where the disturbance of the normal state is sudden, and the restoration gradual and difficult, the opposite results are produced; as may be observed in the case of cuts or burns in the body.[44]

### Tastes (65b-66c)

Some account has now been given of the common affections of the body as a whole and of the names bestowed on the agents that produce them; we have next to explain, if we can, the affections that occur in special organs of our bodies and, on the other side, how they are caused by the agents concerned.

First, then, we must make clear to the best of our power what we omitted earlier in speaking of flavors,[45] namely, the affections peculiar to the tongue. These, like most of the others indeed, appear to be due to contractions and dilations of some sort; and further they have more to do than any of the rest with degrees of roughness and smoothness. When earth particles, making their way in at the small veins which serve the tongue as a sort of testing instrument and extend to the heart, come into contact with the moist and soft flesh, as they are melted down they contract and dry up the veins. If

---

[43] The addition of the lower faculties (by implication "mortal") to the "immortal principle" has been mentioned at 42a. The "mortal part of the soul" is mentioned where that passage is recapitulated at 69c, and indeed the expression has already been used at 61c.

[44] Plato here connects his own doctrine of bodily pleasures and pains, most fully set forth in the *Philebus*, with his theory of the particles, whose shapes make them comparatively easy or difficult to dislodge.

[45] χυμός means (1) juice, (2) flavor (residing in a juice), (3) taste (as a sensation). Some references were made to the characteristic flavors of the juices (60a, b) and of the varieties of earth compounds (60e); but nothing was said about the corresponding processes set up in the tongue.

## TASTES

comparatively rough, they are felt as "astringent"; if their roughening effect is slighter, as "harsh."

Substances which rinse the small veins and cleanse the whole region of the tongue are called "acrid," if they produce this effect in excess and attack the substance of the tongue to the point of dissolving some part of it; such is the property of soda. Those which are less powerful than soda and rinse the tongue to a moderate degree are saline without acrid roughness and rather produce an agreeable sensation.   ϵ

Others, which absorb the warmth of the mouth and are softened by it, becoming fiery [46] and in their turn scorching that which heated them, mount upward by virtue of their lightness to the senses in the head, cleaving whatever they encounter. On account of these properties all such substances are called "pungent."   66

Again, there are the particles [47] of substances reduced to a fine texture by decomposition before they make their way into the narrow veins—particles that are duly proportioned both to the earthy and to the airy particles which the veins contain, with the result that they set these in motion and cause them to be churned round one another, and, as they are being churned, to form an enclosure and as particles of one sort find their way inside particles of a different sort, to produce hollow films stretched round those that pass into the inside.[48]

---

[46] There is no inconsistency, if the substances in question (which are not named) contain water or consist mainly of water, like the juices at 59e. The water particles can be transformed into fire. It has not (as Tr. alleges, p. 466) "been assumed all along that things get their flavors from the earthy particles they contain (γήινα μέρη, 65d, 2)." A.-H. instances the effect of mustard.

[47] The requirement seems to be that the entering particles of moisture shall have been reduced by decomposition to a grade fine enough to permit them to fill the interstices between both the earth cubes and the air octahedra in the passages. The nominative is left in suspense.

[48] The construction and meaning are here uncertain. This part of the sentence seems to describe the formation of a bubble by a stirring movement, producing a globular film of moisture enclosing air.

Thus, when a hollow film of moisture, earthy or pure as the
b case may be, is stretched round air, they form, as moist vessels
of air, hollow globes of water. Some, composed of pure
moisture making a transparent enclosure, are called "bubbles"; while, if the moisture is earthy and stirs and rises all
together, we speak of frothing and fermentation. What is responsible for these effects is called "acid."

An affection opposite to all those which have just been
c described is produced by an opposite cause. When the structure of the entering particles in liquids, being conformable to
the normal condition of the tongue, mollifies and smooths the
roughened parts and relaxes or contracts those which are unnaturally shrunken or dilated, and so thoroughly establishes
the normal state, any such remedy for violent affections is
always pleasant and agreeable, and has received the name
"sweet."

## Odors (66d-67a)

d So much for that matter. In the case of the faculty residing
in the nostrils no definite types [49] are to be discerned. A smell
is always a half-formed thing, and no type of figure has the
proportions necessary for having an odor. The veins of smell
have a structure too narrow for earth and water and too wide
for fire and air; hence no one has ever perceived any odor in
any of these bodies; odors arise from substances in process of
e being liquefied or decomposed or dissolved or evaporated.
They occur in the intermediate stage when water is changing
into air or air into water. All odors are vapor or mist, mist
being that which is on the way from air to water; vapor, what
is on the way from water to air; consequently, all odors are
finer than water, grosser than air. Their nature is plainly seen
when a man forcibly inhales the air through something that
obstructs the passage of the breath: then no odor filters
through with it; nothing comes but the air robbed of all scent.

---

[49] εἴδη, definite varieties of smell, which could be classified by names corresponding to "sour," "pungent," "bitter," etc., in tastes. εἴδει in the next line plainly means type of regular figure (pyramid octahedron, etc.).

Accordingly, the diversities of odor fall into two sets. They lack names because they do not consist of a definite number of simple types. The only clear distinction to be drawn here is twofold: the pleasant and the unpleasant. The unpleasant roughens and does violence to the whole cavity lying between the crown of the head and the navel; the pleasant soothes this region and restores it with contentment to its natural state.

## Sounds (67a-c)

Third among the organs of sensation we are considering is hearing; and the affections occurring in this field must now be explained. Sound we may define in general terms as the stroke inflicted by air on the brain and blood through the ears and passed on to the soul; while the motion it causes, starting in the head and ending in the region of the liver, is hearing. A rapid motion produces a high-pitched sound; the slower the motion, the lower the pitch. If the motion is regular, the sound is uniform and smooth; if irregular, the sound is harsh. According as the movement is on a large or a small scale, the sound is loud or soft. Consonance of sounds must be reserved for a later part of our discourse.

## Colors (67c-68d)

There remains yet a fourth kind of sensation which demands classification, since it embraces a great number of diversities. They are known by the general name of color, a flame which streams off from bodies of every sort and has its particles so proportioned to the visual ray as to yield sensation. Earlier we have explained merely how the visual ray arises; so it is natural and fitting to add here a reasonable account of the colors, as follows.

The particles that come from other bodies and enter the visual ray when they encounter it, are sometimes smaller, sometimes larger than those of the visual ray itself; or they may be of the same size. Those of the same size are imperceptible—"transparent," as we call them. The larger, which contract the ray, and the smaller which dilate it, are analogous to what is cold or hot to the flesh, and again to what is astringent or burning ("pungent," as we call it) to the tongue. These are black and white, affections which are due to those particles and are similar in character, though occurring in a different field and for that reason presenting themselves in a different guise. The names should be assigned accordingly: "white" to what dilates the visual ray, "black" to what contracts it.

When the more piercing motion belonging to a different variety of fire falls upon the ray and dilates it right up to the eyes and forcibly thrusts apart and dissolves the very passages in the eyeball, it causes the discharge of a mass of fire and water which we call a tear. Itself consisting of fire, it meets fire from the opposite quarter leaping out like a flash of lightning, while the in-going fire is quenched in the moisture; and in this confusion all manner of colors arise. The effect we call "dazzling"; the agent which produces it "bright" and "flashing." [50]

Then there is the variety of fire intermediate between these two, which reaches the moisture of the eyeball and is mixed with it, but is not flashing. The radiance of the fire through the moisture with which it is mingled yields blood-color, which we call "red."

Bright mixed with red and white produces orange. In what proportions they are mixed it would be foolish to state, even if one could know; the matter is one in which no one could be even moderately sure of giving either a proof or a plausible estimate.

Red blended with black and white is purple, or dark violet, when these ingredients are burned to a further point and more black is added to the mixture.

Tawny is formed by blending orange and gray, gray being

---

[50] "Bright" and "flashing" are ranked as colors. This supports the belief that Greek terms for color have more to do with differences of tone and brilliance than with differences of shade.

a mixture of white and black; while yellow is a combination of white with orange.

White combined with bright and plunged in intense black results in a dark blue color; dark blue mixed with white, in pale blue-green; tawny and black, in green (?).

From these examples it will be sufficiently clear by what combinations the remaining colors should be represented so as to preserve the probability of the account. But any attempt to put these matters to a practical test would argue ignorance of the difference between human nature and divine, namely, that divinity has knowledge and power sufficient to blend the many into one and to resolve the one into many, but no man is now, or ever will be, equal to either task.

### Conclusion (68e-69a)

All these things, then, being so constituted of necessity, were taken over by the maker of the fairest and best of all things that become, when he gave birth to the self-sufficing and most perfect god; he made use of causes of this order as subservient, while he himself contrived the good in all things that come to be. We must accordingly distinguish two kinds of cause, the necessary and the divine. The divine we should search out in all things for the sake of a life of such happiness as our nature admits; the necessary for the sake of the divine, reflecting that apart from the necessary those other objects of our serious study cannot by themselves be perceived or communicated, nor can we in any other way have part or lot in them.

## III. THE CO-OPERATION OF REASON AND NECESSITY

The third part now opens with a brief recapitulation of the steps by which the account of the works of Reason in the first part led us to the same point that we have now reached once more, from the opposite quarter, in the analysis of what happens of Necessity: namely, the point of contact between the individual soul and the external world in sensation and sense perception. In the first part the rational soul was framed by the Demiurge himself. The second part has analyzed the bodily down to its foundation in Space, the Receptacle of all becoming, and then built it up again by introducing the element of regular geometrical shape, imposed upon the chaotic motions and powers. The interaction of the simple bodies so formed has been described mainly in terms of necessary causation with little reference to rational design. The third part is now to exhibit the co-operation of Reason and Necessity in the work of the created gods. Their task is to frame the mortal parts of the soul and the bodily organs to house them. Henceforward the interest of intelligent purpose again predominates. The distinction between the created gods and the Demiurge is not maintained. Throughout this last part of the dialogue, the work is done sometimes by "the gods," sometimes by "the god"; at one place (71a) plural and singular are used in the same sentence. Plato does not seriously mean that the divine souls of the stars take an active part in the making of other living creatures. Their creative function is as mythical as that of the Demiurge, from which it is no longer kept distinct.

## *Recapitulation. Addition of the mortal parts of soul* (69a-d)

Now that the materials for our building lie ready sorted to our hand, namely the kinds of cause we have distinguished, which are to be combined in the fabric of our remaining discourse, let us in brief return to our starting point and rapidly trace the steps that led us to the point from which we have now reached the same position once more;[1] and then attempt
b to crown our story with a completion fitting all that has gone before.

As was said at the outset, these things were in disorder and the god introduced into them all every kind of measure in

---

[1] The "same position" is sensation and sense-perception, which we reached at the end of the first part (45b–47e), and have now reached again in the concluding paragraphs of the second part. The expression is condensed; but ταὐτόν can hardly bear any other meaning.

every respect in which it was possible for each one to be in harmonious proportion both with itself and with all the rest. For at first they were without any such proportion, save by mere chance,[2] nor was there anything deserving to be called by the names we now use—fire, water, and the rest; but all these he first set in order, and then framed out of them this universe, a single living creature containing within itself all c living creatures, mortal and immortal. Of the divine he himself undertook to be the maker; the task of making the generation of mortals he laid upon his own offspring. They, imitating him, when they had taken over an immortal principle of soul, went on to fashion for it a mortal body englobing it round about.[3] For a vehicle they gave it the body as a whole, and therein they built on another form of soul, the mortal, having in itself dread and necessary affections: first pleasure, d the strongest lure of evil; next, pains that take flight from good; temerity, moreover, and fear, a pair of unwise counselors; passion hard to entreat, and hope too easily led astray. These they combined with irrational sense and desire that shrinks from no venture, and so of necessity[4] compounded the mortal element.

[2] The reference is to those transient semblances of order which might occur without design in the chaos described at 53a by the mere attraction of like to like, or in the Atomists' casual vortices, or in Empedocles' system by the elements rushing through one another (cf. Ar., *Phys.* B4, 196a, 20 ff.).

[3] The head, the "spherical body" in which the revolutions of the immortal soul were confined (44d). The trunk and limbs were then added as a "vehicle" to carry the head about. Cf. 73c, the god molds the brain containing "the divine seed" into a spherical ball.

[4] Note ἀναγκαίως here and ἀναγκαῖα παθήματα above (c). The words echo the repeated references to necessity in the parallel passage (42a) here specially referred to. The body and the concomitant desires and passions of the mortal soul are a necessary (indispensable) adjunct to the immortal part, if man is to exist on earth. Limited by this necessity, the gods have now to establish the mortal soul, as best they can, in suitable organs.

## The bodily seats of the two mortal parts of the soul (69d-72d)

*Two groups of organs corresponding to the mortal parts of the soul.*

Now fearing, no doubt, to pollute the divine part on their account, save in so far as was altogether necessary, they housed the mortal apart from it in a different dwelling place in the body, building between head and breast, as an isthmus and boundary, the neck, which they placed between to keep the two apart. In the breast, then, and the trunk (as it is called) they confined the mortal kind of soul. And since part of it has a nobler nature, part a baser, they built another partition across the hollow of the trunk, as if marking off the men's apartment from the women's, and set the midriff as a fence between them.

## The Spirited part situated in the heart. The lungs

That part of the soul, then, which is of a manly spirit and ambitious of victory they housed nearer to the head, between the midriff and the neck, that it might be within hearing of the discourse of reason and join with it in restraining by force the desires, whenever these should not willingly consent to obey the word of command from the citadel. The heart, then, the knot of the veins and the fountain of the blood which moves impetuously round throughout all the members,[5] they established in the guardroom, in order that, when the spirit should boil with anger at a message from reason that some act of wrong is taking place in the members, whether coming

---

[5] Cf. [Hippocr.] π. καρδίης, 7: the great artery and the thick vein are the fountains of man's nature, and the rivers by which the body is watered. They carry the life of man, and if they are dried up, he dies. From the many points of contact between this treatise and Plato and Diocles, Wellmann concludes that it was written under the influence of the Sicillian medical school and in particular of Philistion (*ibid.*, 107).

from outside or, it may be, from the desires within, then every sentient part of the body should quickly, through all the narrow channels, be made aware of the commands and threats and hearken with entire obedience, and so suffer the noblest part to be leader among them all.

Moreover, for the throbbing of the heart when danger is foreseen or anger aroused, foreseeing that all such swelling of passion would come to pass by means of fire, they devised a relief by implanting the structure of the lung, soft and bloodless and moreover perforated within by cavities like a sponge, in order that by receiving breath and drink, it might cool the heart and so provide refreshment and ease in the burning. For this purpose they cut the channels of the windpipe to reach the lung, and set the lung itself around the heart as a sort of buffer, so that, when the spirit therein was at the height of passion, the heart might leap against a yielding substance and be cooled down, and so, being in less distress, be the better able to help the spirited element in the service of reason.

*The Appetitive part situated in the belly. The liver and the spleen*

That part of the soul whose appetite is set on meat and drink and all that it has need of for the sake of the body's nature, they housed between the midriff and the boundary toward the navel, constructing in all this region as it were a manger for the body's nourishment. There they tethered it like a beast untamed but necessary to be maintained along with the rest if a mortal race were ever to exist. Accordingly, they stationed it here with the intent that, always feeding at its stall and dwelling as far as possible from the seat of counsel, it might cause the least possible tumult and clamor and allow the highest part to take thought in peace for the common profit of each and all.

And because they knew that it would not understand the discourse of reason and that, even if it should somehow become aware of any such discourse, it would not be in its nature to take any heed, whereas it would most readily fall under the spell of images and phantoms both by night and by day, the god, designing to gain this very influence, formed the liver and set it in the creature's dwelling place, and contrived that it should be a substance close in texture, smooth and bright, possessing both sweetness and bitterness. The purpose was that the influence proceeding from the reason should make impressions of its thoughts upon the liver, which would receive them like a mirror and give back visible images. This influence would strike terror into the appetitive part at such times as, taking a part in keeping with the liver's bitterness, it threatens with stern approach; swiftly suffusing this bitterness throughout the liver, it would cause bilious colors to appear thereon; make it all rough and wrinkled by contraction; and as it shrinks and bows down the lobe, obstructs the vessels, and closes the entrance, produce pain and nausea. Sometimes, again, when some inspiration of gentleness from the mind delineates semblances of the contrary sort, it gives rest from the bitterness, because it will not stir up or have dealings with a nature contrary to its own; rather, using toward it a sweetness of like nature to the sweetness in the liver itself, and setting it right till all is straight and smooth and free, it makes that part of the soul that dwells in the region of the liver [6] to thrive in well-being and gentleness of mood, and by night to pass its time in the sober exercise of divination by dreams, since it had no part in rational discourse and understanding. For our makers remembered their father's injunction to make the mortal race as perfect as possible, and they tried to set even the baser part of us on the right path in this way, by establishing the seat of divination in this part, that it might have some apprehension of reality and truth.

That divination is the gift of heaven to human unwisdom

[6] This phrase might support Galen's often repeated assertion that Plato regards the liver as the seat of the appetitive part.

we have good reason to believe, in that no man in his normal senses deals in true and inspired divination, but only when the power of understanding is fettered in sleep or he is distraught by some disorder or, it may be, by divine possession. It is for the man in his ordinary senses to recall and construe the utterances, in dream or in waking life, of divination or possession, and by reflection to make out in what manner and to whom all the visions of the seer betoken some good or ill, past, present, or to come. When a man has fallen into frenzy and is still in that condition, it is not for him to determine the meaning of his own visions and utterances; rather the old saying is true, that only the sound in mind can attend to his own concerns and know himself. Hence it is the custom to set up spokesmen to pronounce judgment on inspired divination. These are themselves given the name of diviners by some who are quite unaware that they are expositors of riddling oracle or vision and best deserve to be called, not diviners, but spokesmen of those who practice divination.

This, then, is the reason why the liver has such a nature and situation as we have described: it is for the sake of divination. So long as any creature is yet alive the indications given by such an organ are comparatively clear;[7] but deprived of life it becomes blind and its signs are too dim to convey any certain meaning.

Again, the structure of the neighboring organ and its position on the left are for the sake of the liver, to keep it always bright and clean, like a napkin provided to wipe a mirror and always laid ready beside it. So, when any impurities arise in the region of the liver from bodily disorders, they are all purged away and absorbed by the spleen, whose texture is not close, since it has cavities not containing blood. Hence,

---

[7] The words ἑκάστου τὸ τοιοῦτον seem intended to include the *corresponding* organ in *any* (nonhuman) creature; for the rest of the sentence dismisses divination from the appearance of the liver in sacrificed animals, although their dream images could not be due to any influence from reason, which they do not possess.

d when it is filled with these offscourings, it waxes swollen and festered, and, when the body is purged, subsides again and is reduced to its former state.

*Summary and transition to the rest of the body* (72d-73a)

Concerning the soul, then, we have stated what part of it is mortal and what divine, and where, in what company, and for what reasons the two are housed apart. We could confidently assert that our account is the truth only if it were first confirmed by heaven; but that it is the probable account we may venture to say now, and still more on further consideration. Let that claim, then, be taken as made.

e The next part of our task must be pursued on the same principles: this was the manner in which the remainder of the body came to be. Now the design that would most fittingly account for its construction would be this. The framers of mankind knew what would be our intemperance in meat and drink and that, out of gluttony, we should use far more than the moderate or necessary amount. Accordingly, to make provision against the danger that disease should bring swift destruction and the mortal race should forthwith
73 come to an end in immaturity, they appointed the lower belly (as it is called) as a receptacle to hold the superfluity of food and drink, and wound the bowels round in coils, in order that the nourishment should not pass so quickly through as to constrain the body to crave fresh nourishment too soon, and thus, making it insatiable, render all mankind incapable, through gluttony, of all cultivation and philosophy, deaf to the command of the divinest part of our nature.

*The main structure of the human frame* (73b-76e)

*The marrow, seed, and brain*

b With bone, flesh, and all substances of that sort the case stands thus. The starting point for all these was the formation of the marrow, for the bonds of life, so long as the soul is bound up with the body, were made fast in it as the roots of the mortal creature; while the marrow itself is formed of other things. The god set apart from their several kinds those triangles which, being unwarped and smooth, were originally able to produce fire, water, air, and earth of the most exact form.[8] Mixing these in due proportion to one another, he made out of them the marrow, contriving thus a mixture of seeds of every sort for every mortal kind. Next he implanted and made fast therein the several kinds of souls; also from the first, in his original distribution, he divided the marrow into shapes corresponding in number and fashion to those which the several kinds were destined to wear. And he molded into spherical shape the plowland, as it were, that was to contain the divine seed; and this part of the marrow he named "brain," [9] signifying that, when each living creature was completed, the vessel containing this should be the head. That part, on the other hand, which was to retain [10] the remaining, mortal, kind of soul he divided into shapes at once round and elongated, naming them all "marrow." [11] From these, as if from anchors, he put forth bonds to fasten all the soul; and now began to fashion our whole body round this thing, first framing round the whole of it a solid shield of bone.

[8] No physical bodies in the visible world of becoming can have the exact perfection of the surfaces and solids of mathematics. This is one of the limiting conditions which prevent the works of Reason from reaching ideal perfection. The triangles composing the surfaces of visible and tangible bodies are only copies of the triangles whose construction was described earlier.

[9] "Brain" (ἐγκέφαλον) because "in the head" (ἐν κεφαλῇ).

[10] The marrow is the life substance in which all parts of the soul are rooted; but it is the actual seat only of the immortal part. The mortal part is located elsewhere, in heart and belly, and only linked to the marrow by anchor cables.

[11] "Shapes," plural, because there are columns of marrow in other bones than the spine.

*Bone, flesh, sinews*

e   And bone he constructed as follows. Having sifted out earth that was pure and smooth, he kneaded it and soaked it with marrows; then he plunged the stuff into fire, next dipped it in water, and again in fire and once more in water; by thus shifting it several times from one to the other he made it insoluble by either. Of this, then, he made use, first to turn a sphere of bone to surround the creature's brain, and to this sphere he left a narrow outlet; and further to surround the
74  marrow along the neck and back, he molded out of bone vertebrae, which he set to serve as pivots, starting from the head through the whole extent of the trunk. Thus, to protect all the seed, he fenced it in a stony enclosure, and in this he made joints, availing himself in their case of the property of the Different, inserted between them [12] for the sake of movement and bending.

Again, considering that the constitution of bone was unduly
b  brittle and inflexible, and moreover that, if it should become fiery hot and then cold again, it would decay and quickly cause the destruction of the seed within it, for these reasons he devised the sinews and the flesh in such a way that, by binding together all the limbs with sinew contracting and relaxing about their sockets, he might enable the body to bend or stretch itself out; while the flesh was to be a defense against burning heat and a shelter from wintry cold, and also a protection against falls, like our borrowed trappings of felt:
c  it would yield to bodies softly and gently, and it contained in itself a warm moisture, which in summer it might sweat forth and so spread a native coolness all over the body by moisten-

---

[12] The spine is unlike the skull in consisting of *many* separate parts and being capable of *variable* movements in any direction. The curious phrase indicates that Plato saw something symbolic in this contrast with the single and solid sphere of the skull analogous to the spherical body of the world, adapted only to the constant revolutions of the rational soul. The lower parts of the soul, connected with the spinal marrow, exhibit the characteristics of the "wandering cause."

ing it outside, while in winter, on the other hand, we should have this fire as a fair protection against the assaults of the beleaguering frost outside. With this intent, he who molded us like wax composed flesh, soft and full of sap, by making a duly adjusted compound with water and fire and earth, which he suffused with a ferment composed of acid and saline. The sinews, again, he made by mixing bone with unfermented flesh into a substance with properties intermediate between those two constituents, adding a yellow color; hence the sinews acquired a quality more tense and consistent than flesh, but softer and more pliable than bone. With these the god enveloped the bones and marrow, binding the bones to one another with sinews, and he then buried them all under a covering of flesh.

*The uneven distribution of flesh*

Now those bones in which there is most life he fenced about with the smallest amount of flesh; those having least life within them, with flesh in the greatest abundance and of the toughest kind; moreover at the joints of the bones, wherever no cogent reason appeared to require it, he caused but little flesh to grow. The purpose was that flesh should not hamper the bending of the joints and so stiffen the body as to make it hard to move about; and, secondly, that the solidity of many layers of thick flesh packed close on one another should not cause dullness of sensation and produce hardness of apprehension and unretentiveness in the quarters of the mind. For this reason the thighs and shins and parts about the hips, the bones of the upper arms and forearms, and all other parts where there are no joints, and also all the bones within the body that are devoid of intelligence because they have so little soul residing in marrow—all these have a full complement of flesh. Those parts, on the contrary, which are the seat of intelligence have less—save where he formed a mass of flesh to be in itself an organ of sensation, as for instance the structure of the tongue. With most parts, however, it is as afore-

said; for the constitution of this frame which of necessity
b comes into being and is reared with us in no wise allows dense
bone and much flesh to go together with keenly responsive
sensation. For if these two characters had consented to coincide, the structure of the head would have possessed them
above all, and the human race, bearing a head fortified with
flesh and sinew, would have enjoyed a life twice or many times
as long as now, healthier and more free from pain. But as it
was, the artificers who brought us into being reckoned
whether they should make a long-lived but inferior race or
c one with a shorter life but nobler, and agreed that everyone
must on all accounts prefer the shorter and better life to the
longer and worse. Hence they covered in the head with thin
bone, but not with flesh nor yet with sinews, since it has no
flexions. Accordingly the head they attached to the body of
every man is all the more sensitive and intelligent, but much
weaker. The sinews, again, on the same principle and for
d these reasons, were set by the god all round the neck so far as
to the base of the head and welded by means of uniformity,
and he fastened to them the extremities of the jawbones just
under the face; while the rest he distributed among all the
limbs, connecting the joints. The mouth was equipped by
our makers for its office with teeth, tongue, and lips arranged
as now, for the sake at once of what is necessary and what
is best. They devised it as the passage whereby necessary
e things might enter and the best things pass out; for all that
comes in to give sustenance to the body is necessary; but the
outflowing stream of discourse, ministering to intelligence, is
of all streams the best and noblest.

*Skin, hair, nails*

The head, however, could not be left merely of bare bone
because of the extremes of heat and cold in the seasons; nor
yet could they suffer it to be so muffled in masses of flesh as
to become insensitive and dull. So from the flesh, which was
76 not entirely dried up in the process, there was separated a

film which was superfluously large—"skin" as we now call it. This, owing to the moisture in the brain, grew and closed in on itself so as to clothe the head all round; and the moisture rising up under the sutures watered it and closed it, like a knot drawn together, on the crown. The sutures are of very various patterns due to the action of the revolutions and of the nutriment, being more or fewer in number according as the struggle between those powers is more or less intense.[13]

Now this skin was pricked all round with fire by the divine part;[14] and when the moisture issued forth through the holes pierced in it, all that was purely moist and hot passed away, but the part that was compounded of the same ingredients as the skin was lifted by the motion and stretched into a long thread outside, of a fineness equal in size to the puncture; but its movement was so slow that it was thrust back by the surrounding air without and coiling back inside under the skin took root there. To these processes is due all the hair that grows on the skin: it is a thread-shaped substance of the same nature as the skin, but harder and denser as a result of the felting effect of the cooling, whereby each hair is felted together as it is detached from the skin. When our creator made our heads shaggy with it, he used the means above stated, but his thought was that this was the right thing to serve, instead of flesh, as a covering to protect the brain, both light and sufficient to provide shade in summer and shelter in winter, without being an obstacle to hinder readiness of perception.

Further, where the fabric of sinew, skin, and bone is finished off in fingers and toes, a compound of the three, when it is dried off, forms a single hard skin containing them all. Such were the means used in its making, but the true reason and purpose of the work was for the sake of creatures that

---

[13] The conflict which goes on in infancy, 43a ff. In this paragraph and the two following the operation of "Necessity" comes to the front and Plato speaks as if skin, hair, and nails had been developed by the blind action of the primary bodies, unconsciously subserving a useful purpose.

[14] The fire in the brain, forcing its way upwards to seek its like.

were to be hereafter. For our framers knew that some day men would pass into women and also into beasts, and that many creatures [15] would need nails (claws and hoofs) for many purposes; hence they designed the rudiments of this growth from the very birth of mankind.

Such, then, were their reasons and purposes in causing the growth of skin, hair, and nails at the extremities of the limbs.

## Plants (76e-77c)

Now that all the parts and limbs of the mortal creature were united in a living whole, which, as the result of necessity, must spend his life surrounded by fire and air and be consequently dissolved and depleted by them and so waste away, the gods devised succor for him. They gave birth to a substance of a kindred nature to man's, but combined with other shapes and senses, so as to be a living creature of a different sort. These are trees, plants, and seeds, now tamed and schooled by husbandry into domestication with us, though formerly there were only the wild kinds, which are the older. Anything that has life has every right to be called a living creature in the proper sense; and the kind of which we are now speaking has the third form of soul, which, we said, is seated between midriff and navel; this has nothing to do with belief or with reasoning and understanding, but only with sensation, pleasant or painful, and appetites. For it is always suffering all affections, but its formation has not endowed it with any power to observe the nature of its own affections and to reflect thereon by revolving within and about itself, rejecting motion from without and exercising motion of its

---

[15] Beasts (not women), as Galen rightly understood (*U.P.* 1, 121). Plato is neither anticipating Darwin nor following Empedocles. Women and beasts have not actually developed from men; nor had anyone ever believed that they did. But Plato, having included transmigration in his mythical machinery, with the unusual and fantistic addition that men are imagined as existing at first alone, has to take this way of conveying that claws and hoofs in animals are more obviously useful to them than nails are to human beings.

own. Therefore it lives, indeed, and is no other than a living creature, but it stands still, fixed and rooted, because it is denied self-motion.[16]

*Irrigation system to convey nourishment. The two principal veins (77c-e)*

Now when the higher powers had planted all these kinds as sustenance for our nature, weaker than their own, they made throughout the body itself a system of conduits, cut like runnels in a garden, so that it might be, as it were, watered by an incoming stream. First they cut as covered conduits, under the juncture of skin and flesh, two veins along the back corresponding to the twofold form of the body, with a right side and a left. These they brought down alongside the spine, enclosing between them also the generative marrow, in order that this might be kept in full vigor and also that, by running downhill, the current might flow easily thence to the other parts and make the irrigation uniform.

Next, they split up these veins in the region of the head and plaited the ends so as to pass across one another in opposite directions, slanting those from the right toward the left side of the body and those from the left toward the right side. This was partly to provide the head with a bond helping the skin to connect it with the body, since there were no sinews holding it all round at the crown,[17] and further in order that the body as a whole might be informed of the effect of sense-perceptions coming from the members on either side.[18]

---

[16] Not all self-motion, since it has soul which is by definition the self-moving thing. Only motion from place to place is meant. As Galen remarks (*Comment.* p. 12, Daremberg), plants can grow upward and downward and attract nourishment.

[17] The sinews stopped short at the base of the skull (75d).

[18] We learned at 70b that the blood, rushing outward from the heart when anger boils up, conveys to all sentient parts a message from the brain, which has been warned by perception of some injury needing retaliation.

## Respiration as the driving power of the irrigation system (77e-79a)

They then proceeded to provide for the water-carrying in a manner now to be described, which we shall the more easily grasp if we first agree upon the following principle. All bodies composed of smaller particles are impervious to larger particles, but those consisting of the larger are not impervious to the smaller; and of all the kinds fire has the smallest particles and consequently passes through water, earth, and air and all bodies composed of these, and nothing is impervious to it. This principle must be applied to our belly: [19] when food and drink fall into it, it keeps them in; but it cannot keep in the air we breathe and fire, since their particles are smaller than those of its own structure.

## The Weel or Fish-trap

The god accordingly made use of these (air and fire) for the water-carrying from the belly to the veins, weaving out of air and fire a network, after the fashion of a fisherman's weel. This had a pair of funnels (ἐγκύρτια) at the entrance, one of which again he made fork into two; and from these funnels he stretched, as it were, reeds all round throughout the whole length to the extremities of the network. The whole interior of the basket he composed of fire, while the funnels and the main vessel were of air.

This structure he took and set it about the living creature he had molded, in this way. The part consisting of the funnels he let into the mouth; and this part being twofold, he prolonged [20] one of the funnels downward by way of the wind-

---

[19] Here and below κοιλία probably means, not the whole hollow of the trunk, but the belly, where fire reduces meat and drink to blood (80d). Plato is specially thinking of this as the first operation, which must be performed before the blood is driven upward (see 78e–79a). It is of course also true that fire and air can penetrate the skin anywhere.

[20] It should be remembered that the lung contains no blood (70c). Its passages are filled with air and fire.

pipes into the lung, and the other alongside the windpipes into the belly. The first funnel he divided into two parts, to both of which he gave a common outlet by the channels of the nose,[21] so that when the other passage was not working by way of the mouth, all its currents also might be replenished from this one. The rest, the main vessel of the weel, he at- d tached round all the hollow part of the body. And all this he caused at one moment to flow together inward onto the funnels—softly, because they are made of air; while at another moment the funnels flow back, and the network sinks in through the body—for this is porous—and then out again; meanwhile the rays of fire stretched through inside follow the movement of the air in either direction. This process was to continue without ceasing so long as the mortal creature holds e together; it is indeed the process which the name-giver entitled inhalation and exhalation.

All this that our body does and has done to it results in its being nourished and keeping alive as it is watered and cooled; for every time that, as the breath passes in and out, the fire within connected with it follows its movement and in its perpetual rise and fall passes in through the belly and takes hold upon the meat and drink, it dissolves them and, dividing 79 them up small, drives them through the outlets in the direction of its advance, discharging them into the veins, as water from a spring into runnels, and making the currents of the veins flow through the body as through an aqueduct.

### *Respiration maintained by the circular thrust* (79a-e)

But let us once more consider the means whereby the effect of respiration has come to take place as it now does. It was in this way. Since there is no vacancy into which any moving b body could make its way, and the air we breathe does move

---

[21] The breath funnel was originally forked into two passages, the mouth and the nose (78b). I understand the present operation to be the splitting of the nose passage into the two nostrils (so A.-H.). This completes the system of passages.

out from us, the consequence is at once plain to anyone: it does not go out into vacancy, but thrusts the neighboring air out of its place. What is so thrust keeps on displacing its neighbors successively, and in the course of this compulsion the air is all driven round and enters the place whence the breath came out, refilling it as it follows the breath. All this goes on simultaneously,[22] as when a wheel is driven round,

c because there is no vacancy. Consequently, the region of the chest and lung, in the act of discharging the breath outward, is filled again by the air surrounding the body, as it is driven round and makes its way inward through the porous flesh. Again, when the air is turned back and is moving outward through the body, it thrusts round the respiration inward by way of the passage of mouth and nostrils.

We must suppose that the starting of this process is to be explained as follows. In every living creature the inner parts

d about the blood and veins are the hottest, like a fountain of fire which it has within itself.[23] It was, indeed, this that we likened to the network of our weel, when we said that the whole extent of the central part was woven of fire, while all the parts on the outside were of air. Now we must agree that the hot naturally moves outward toward its kindred in its own region; and that, since there are two ways through, one leading out by way of the body, while the other is by way of

e mouth and nostrils, whenever the hot makes for the air in one quarter, it gives a thrust round to the air in the other quarter; and the air so thrust round, falling into the fire, is heated, while the air which passes out is cooled.

And as the warmth changes and the air which travels by way of the one outlet gets warmer, the warmer air is the more inclined to take the reverse direction by that route, moving toward its like, and gives a circular thrust to the air which

---

[22] Not leaving any interval of time during which there would be a space left unfilled.

[23] Presumably the principal seat of this fountain of fire in blood and veins is the heart, "the knot of the veins and the fountain of blood," whose throbbing when it swells with passion is "caused by fire" (70a-c).

travels by the other passage. This again suffers the same effect and reacts every time in the same way. So it sets up, under the two impulses, a motion like that of a wheel which swings now this way, now that, and thus it gives rise to inhalation and exhalation.

## *Digression. Other phenomena explained by the circular thrust* (79e-80c)

Plato now interrupts his account of the irrigation system by a short digression. The principle of the circular thrust will help to explain a number of other phenomena, which had been falsely supposed to involve the existence of void or of a power of "attraction" which Plato will not recognize.

To this principle, moreover, we may look for the explanation of what happens in the cases of medical instruments for cupping, of the process of swallowing, and of projectiles, which keep moving after their discharge either through the air or along the ground. 80

This principle will also explain why sounds, which present themselves as high or low in pitch according as they are swift or slow, are as they travel sometimes inharmonious because the motion they produce in us lacks correspondence, sometimes concordant because there is correspondence. The slower sounds, when they catch up with the motions of the quicker sounds which arrived earlier, find these motions drawing to an end and already having reached correspondence with the motions imparted to them by the slower sounds on their later arrival. In so doing, the slower sounds cause no disturbance when they intrude a fresh motion; rather by joining on the beginning of a slower motion in correspondence with the quicker which is now drawing to an end, they produce a single combined effect in which high and low are blended. Hence the pleasure they give to the unintelligent, and the delight they afford to the wise, by the representation of the divine harmony in mortal movements. b

There are, moreover, the flowing of any stream of water, the falling of thunderbolts, and the "attraction" of amber and of the loadstone at which men wonder. There is no real attraction in any of these cases. Proper investigation will make it plain that there is no void; that the things in question thrust themselves round, one upon another; that the several kinds of body, as they are disintegrated or put together, all interchange the regions toward which they move; and that the results which seem magical are due to the complication of these effects.

*How blood is formed by digestion and conveyed through the veins. Growth and decay. Natural death (80d-81e)*

Now the effect of respiration, whence this discussion arose, takes place, as we said before, on this principle and by these means: the fire cuts up our food and oscillates inside us as it accompanies the breath; and by thus oscillating with it, fills the veins from the belly by discharging the cut-up food from thence. By this means, in any animal, the streams of nourishment are kept flowing throughout the whole body. The particles, being freshly divided and coming from kindred substances—from fruits or herbs which the god caused to grow for this very purpose of feeding us—take on all manner of colors owing to their being mixed together; but they are chiefly pervaded by a red hue, a character inwrought on moisture by fire that cuts and stains it.[24] Hence the color of the stream throughout the body assumes the appearance we have described; this we call blood, on which the flesh and the whole body feed, so that every member draws water therefrom to replenish the base of the depleted part.[25] The manner of this replenishment and wasting is like that movement of all things in the universe which carries each thing toward its own kind.

---

[24] Cf. the account of red or blood color at 68b.

[25] τὴν τοῦ κενουμένου βάσιν, not "the places that are left void" (A.-H.). The main food-conveying channels of the blood are sunk deep within the flesh, which is watered and fed from beneath, as a plant from its roots.

For the elements besetting us outside are always dissolving and distributing our substance, spending each kind of body on its way to join its fellows; while on the other hand the substances in the blood, when they are broken up small within us and find themselves comprehended by the individual living creature, framed like a heaven to include them,[26] are con-  b
strained to reproduce the movement of the universe. Thus each substance within us that is reduced to fragments replenishes at once the part that has just been depleted by moving toward its own kind.

*Normal growth and decay*

Now whenever there is more going out than flowing in, all things diminish; when there is less, they grow. So when the frame of the whole creature is young and the triangles of its constituent bodies are still as it were fresh from the workshop, their joints are firmly locked together, although the consistency of the whole bulk is soft, having been but lately formed of marrow and nourished on milk. Accordingly, since  c
any triangles composing the meat and drink, which come in from outside and are enveloped within the young creature, are older and weaker than its own, with its new-made triangles it gets the better of them and cuts them up, and so causes the animal to wax large, nourishing it with an abundance of substances like its own.[27] But when the root [28] of the

---

[26] An allusion to 58a, which explained how all the four primary bodies are comprehended by "the circuit of the whole," and how mutual attraction of likes and the constant changes of direction of transformed bodies keep the whole together and tend to allow no vacancy to be left unfilled. The movement is reproduced here in the microcosm.

[27] The doctrine that each substance in our body is nourished by the accession of like substances already present in our food and drink was clearly asserted by Anaxagoras, and is alluded to at *Phaedo* 96d. Cf. Ar., *de gen. et corr.* 333[b], 1 (Empedocles).

[28] ἡ ῥίζα τῶν τριγώνων χαλᾷ. This curious metaphor must describe the opposite of what was called above "being strongly locked together" (σύγκλεισιν) so as to form a firm solid. This favors Tr.'s view (p. 586) that

triangles is loosened by reason of the many conflicts in which they have long been engaged with so many others, they can
d no longer cut up into their own likeness the triangles of the nourishment as they enter, but are themselves easily divided by the intruders from without. So every living creature is at this time overmastered and wastes away; and this condition is called old age.

And at last, when the conjoined bonds of the triangles in the marrow no longer hold out under the stress, but part asunder, they let go in their turn the bonds of the soul;[29] and she, when thus set free in the course of nature, finds pleasure in taking wing to fly away. For whereas all that is
e against nature is painful, what takes place in the natural way is pleasant. So death itself, on this principle, is painful and contrary to nature when it results from disease or wounds, but when it comes to close the natural course of old age, it is, of all deaths, the least distressing and is accompanied rather by pleasure than by pain.

## Diseases of the body (81e-86a)

### (1) *Diseases due to excess or defect or misplacement of the primary bodies*

The origin of diseases is no doubt evident to all.. Since
82 there are four kinds which compose the body, earth, fire, water, and air, disorders and diseases arise from the un-

---

"roots" means the sides, which are the lines along which triangles are joined to compose a corpuscle. The metaphor seems to be taken from the loosening of a tree's roots. I cannot see that ῥίζα has anything to do with a ship, as Tr. would have it. The only phrase in the whole context that definitely suggests a ship is ἐκ δρυόχων; but that was a current metaphor applied to other things.

[29] At 89b we learn that each individual has his allotted span of life, "since the triangles in every creature are from the outset put together with the power to hold out for a certain time, beyond which life cannot be prolonged."

natural prevalence or deficiency of these, or from their migration from their own proper place to an alien one; or again, since there are several varieties of fire and the rest, from any bodily part's taking in an unsuitable variety, and from all other causes of this kind. For when any one of the kinds is formed or shifts its place contrary to nature, parts that were formerly cold are heated, the dry become moist, and so also b with the light and the heavy, and they undergo changes of every kind. The only way, as we hold, in which any part can be left unchanged and sound and healthy is that the same thing should be coming to it and departing from it with constant observance of uniformity and due proportion; any element that trespasses beyond these limits in its incoming or passing out will give rise to a great variety of alterations and to diseases and corruptions without number.

(2) *Diseases of the (secondary) tissues*

Again, seeing that secondary formations exist in nature, an attentive consideration will discern a second class of diseases. c Since marrow, bone, flesh, and sinew are composed of the bodies above named, and blood also of the same bodies, though in a different way, most of the diseases affecting them arise in the same manner as those just mentioned; but the most serious afflictions take the form of a corruption of these structures, which occurs when the process of their formation is reversed.

In the natural course flesh and sinews arise from the blood —sinew from fibrine (for they are cognate), flesh from the compacting of the blood from which the fibrine is being d removed.[30] From sinews and flesh, again, proceeds the viscous

---

[30] It is not explained what agency in the living body causes the blood without fibrine to be compacted into flesh. It may be the "innate heat," for when the blood is cold in the dead body blood without fibrine remains liquid (85d). This is in accordance with the view which Diocles is presumed to have shared with Empedocles that the male embryo is more quickly formed than the female, because the male is in the right (warmer)

and oily stuff which glues the flesh to the structure of the bones and also feeds the growth of the bone itself which encloses the marrow; while at the same time the purest part, consisting of triangles of the smoothest and most slippery sort, filters through the close texture of the bones and, as it is distilled from them in drops, waters the marrow. When the several structures are formed in this order, the result, as a rule, is health.

Disease comes when the order is reversed. Thus, when flesh is decomposed and discharges the results of its decomposition back into the veins, these are then filled with much blood of every sort together with air; this has a diversity of colors and bitternesses, as well as acid and saline qualities, and develops bile, serum, and phlegm of all sorts. All these products of breaking down and corruption in the first place destroy the blood itself, and providing the body with no further nourishment from themselves, they are carried everywhere through the veins, no longer observing the order of natural circulation. They are at feud among themselves because they can get no good of one another; and they make war upon whatsoever in the body keeps orderly array and stays at its post; so they spread corruption and dissolution.

Now when the flesh which is decomposed has been formed a long time before, it resists concoction; it turns black under long exposure to burning, and, being bitter because it is eaten through and through, it is dangerous in its assault upon any part of the body that is as yet uncorrupted. Sometimes, when the bitter stuff has been fined down, the bitterness is replaced by acidity in the black color. Sometimes, again, when the bitterness is steeped in blood it acquires a redder hue, and the mixture of the black with this redness gives it the "bilious" color. Or again, a yellow color may be combined with the bitterness when the flesh decomposed by the fire of the inflammation is of recent formation. To all these the common

---

part of the uterus. Diocles also held that overheating *thickens* the blood and so blocks the veins, causing indigestion. Wellmann, P.-W. Real Encycl., *s.v.* Diokles, 805–6.

name "bile" has been given, either by physicians, or perhaps c
by someone capable of surveying a number of unlike things
and discerning in them all a single kind deserving a name;
while the several varieties of bile recognized[31] have been
specially defined each according to its color.

The serum of black and acid bile (in contrast to that of
blood, which is a harmless lymph) is dangerous when combined with a saline quality by the action of heat; this is called
acid phlegm. There is also the product resulting from the
decomposition of new and tender flesh, accompanied by air.[32]
This is inflated by air and enveloped in moisture so as to form d
bubbles, individually too small to be seen but becoming
visible in the mass, as the froth so formed makes them appear
white in color. All this decomposition of tender flesh in combination with air we call white phlegm. Freshly forming
phlegm, moreover, itself has a lymph, namely sweat, tears,
and all other such flowing substances that are daily purged e
away.

All these things become agents to produce diseases when
the blood, instead of being replenished in the natural way
from food and drink, takes its increase from the opposite
quarter, contrary to the established use of nature.

Now when the several sorts of flesh are broken down by
diseases, so long as their roots hold firm, the mischief is but
half done, for it still admits of easy recovery. But when that
which binds flesh to bone falls sick and in its turn the stream 84
that is separated off from flesh and sinews no longer serves to
nourish bone and bind the flesh thereto, but instead of being
oily, smooth, and viscous, becomes rough and saline, parched

---

[31] Namely the three species above described: black, "bilious," and yellow. The contrast is between the generic name "bile," and these three names for the species (εἴδη). τἄλλα means the species *as opposed to* the genus; not that there are *other* species than those named. Diogenes of Apollonia and his contemporaries are said to have laid much stress on the color of the complexion as a sign of temperamental humors and a symptom of corresponding diseases (*Vors.* 51a, 29a).

[32] As explained at 84e, air is produced *inside the body* by the decomposition of flesh. Cf. also 82e.

by an unhealthy manner of living, then all the substance so affected crumbles back again up into the flesh and sinews as it comes away from the bones; while the flesh, falling away with it from its roots, leaves the sinews bare and full of brine, and itself falls back again into the current of the blood, to aggravate the disorders before described.[33]

Grievous as these affections of the body are, yet graver are those which go deeper and come when the density of the flesh does not allow the bone to receive enough ventilation. Through moldiness the bone is overheated and decays; no longer taking in its proper food, it goes rather the opposite way and crumbles back into the nourishing fluid; and that again falls into flesh, and the flesh into the blood, thus making the maladies of the parts previously mentioned all more virulent.

Finally, the most desperate case of all is when the substance of the marrow becomes diseased by some deficiency or excess. This produces the most serious and deadly disorders, since the whole substance of the body is forced to flow in a backward course.

### (3) *Diseases due to (a) breath, (b) phlegm, (c) bile. Fevers*

A third class of diseases must be conceived as occurring in three ways: (*a*) from breath, (*b*) from phlegm, or (*c*) from bile.

(*a*) When the lung, whose office is to dispense the breath to the body, is blocked by rheums and affords no clear passages, the breath fails to reach some parts and causes them to putrefy for lack of refreshment; while too much of it passes into other quarters, where it forces its way through the veins and contorts them, dissolves the body, and is intercepted when it reaches the barrier at the center. Thus are caused countless painful disorders, often accompanied by much sweat.

Often, too, when flesh is broken down, air is formed inside

---

[33] At 82e–83a. The more superficial diseases due to corruption of the blood by decomposing flesh are reinforced by these more deeply seated affections of the fluid.

the body and, not being able to make its way out, causes the same torments as those due to breath that has come from outside. These are most severe when the air, gathering and swelling up round the sinews and the small veins there, makes them stretch backward the tendons of the back and the sinews attached to them. From the tension so produced the disorders of course derive their names, tetanus and opisthotonus. A cure is difficult; indeed, such cases are, for the most part, relieved by supervening fevers.

(*b*) White phlegm, when intercepted, is dangerous, because of the air in the bubbles; but if it finds an escape to the surface of the body, is milder, though it disfigures the body by engendering white eruptions and kindred maladies. When it is mixed with black bile and is diffused over the divine circuits in the head so as to throw them into confusion, the visitation, if it comes in sleep, is comparatively mild, but an attack in waking hours is harder to throw off. As an affliction of the sacred part, it deserves its name "sacred disease."

Acid and saline phlegm is the source of all disorders that occur by defluxion; they have received many different names according to the divers regions toward which the fluxion is directed.

(*c*) Inflammations of any part of the body, so called from its being burned or "inflamed," are all due to bile. If the bile finds a vent outward, its seething sends up eruptions of various kinds; if shut up within, it engenders many inflammatory diseases. The worst is when the bile mingles with pure blood and breaks up the proper disposition of the fibrine. This substance is distributed throughout the blood to preserve in it a due proportion of thinness and thickness, in order that heat should not so liquefy it as to make it flow out through the porous texture of the body, nor yet should its excessive density make it too sluggish for ready circulation in the veins. The fibrine, by the composition of its substance, preserves the due mean; even after death when the blood is getting cold, if the fibrine is collected, all the rest of the blood is liquefied; whereas, if the fibrine is left, it quickly congeals the blood with the help of the surrounding coldness. Such being the action of fibrine in the blood, bile, which had its origin as old blood and is now dissolved back again into blood out of flesh, when it enters the blood in small quantities at first, hot and liquid, congeals under the action of the fibrine; and while this is happening and its natural heat is being quenched, it sets up internal chill and shivering. As the bile flows in with fuller tide, however, it overpowers the fibrine with its own hotness and by boiling up shakes it into disarray; and if it proves strong enough to obtain the mastery to the end, it penetrates to the substance of the marrow and in consuming it unlooses the soul from her moorings there and sets her free. When the flow is weaker and the body holds out against dissolution the bile is itself overpowered; then either it is expelled all over the surface of the body, or else, after being thrust through the veins into the lower or upper belly, banished from the body like an exile from a city at civil war, it causes diarrhea, dysentery, and all such disorders.

When the body has fallen sick chiefly through excess of fire, it produces continuous heats and fevers; excess of air causes quotidian fevers; excess of water, tertian, water being more sluggish than air or fire. Excess of earth, which ranks as the most sluggish of all the four, takes a fourfold period for its purgation, and produces quartan fevers which are hard to shake off.

## Disease in the Soul due to defective bodily constitution and to bad nurture (86b-87b)

Such is the manner in which disorders of the body arise; disorders of the soul are caused by the bodily condition in the following way. It will be granted that folly is disorder of the soul; and of folly there are two kinds, madness and stupidity. Accordingly, any affection that brings on either of these must be called a disorder; and among the gravest disorders for the soul we must rank excessive pleasures and pains. When a man is carried away by enjoyment or distracted by pain, in his immoderate haste to grasp the one or to escape the other he can neither see nor hear aright; he is in a frenzy and his capacity for reasoning is then at its lowest. Moreover, when the seed in a man's marrow becomes copious with overflowing moisture like the overabundance of fruitfulness in a tree, he is filled with strong pains of travail and with pleasures no less strong on each occasion (?) in his desires and in their satisfaction; for the most part of his life he is maddened by these intense pleasures and pains; and when his soul is rendered sick and senseless by the body he is commonly held to be not sick but deliberately bad. But the truth is that sexual intemperance is a disorder of the soul arising, to a great extent, from the condition of a single substance [34] which, owing to the porousness of the bones, floods the body with its moisture. We might almost say, indeed, of all that is called incontinence in pleasure that it is not justly made a reproach, as if men were willingly bad. No one is willingly bad; the bad man becomes so because of some faulty habit of body and unenlightened upbringing, and these are unwelcome afflictions that come to any man against his will.

Again, where pains are concerned, the soul likewise derives much badness from the body. When acid and salt phlegms or bitter bilious humors roam about the body and, finding no outlet, are pent up within and fall into confusion by blending the vapor that arises from them with the motion of the soul, they induce all manner of disorders of the soul or greater or less intensity and extent.[35] Making their way to the three seats of the soul, according to the region they severally invade,

---

[34] The marrow, or that part of it which forms the seed, which the bones are not dense enough to retain and keep in its proper consistency. At 82d we learned that the marrow is fed by the fluid which filters through the "dense" substance of bone in drops. If the bones are too porous, the marrow will receive too much liquid, and also escape too freely by the channel which will be described later (91a).

[35] It is conjectured that this doctrine of vapors arising from the humors was held by Philistion and Diocles. See Wellmann, *Fr. d. Gr. Aerzte*, p. 78. Cf. the confusion caused in the soul's revolutions by the mixture of phlegm and black bile, causing epilepsy, 85a.

they beget many divers types of ill temper and despondency, of rashness and cowardice, of dullness and oblivion.[36]

Besides all this, when men of so bad a composition dwell in cities with evil forms of government, where no less evil discourse is held both in public and private, and where, moreover, no course of study that might counteract this poison is pursued from youth upward, that is how all of us who are bad become so, through two causes that are altogether against the will.[37] For these the blame must fall upon the parents rather than the offspring,[38] and upon those who give, rather than those who receive, nurture; nevertheless, a man must use his utmost endeavor by means of education, pursuits, and study to escape from badness and lay hold upon its contrary.

*Disproportion between soul and body, to be remedied by regimen and exercise* (87b-89d)

This subject, however, belongs to another kind of discourse; here it is natural and fitting to set forth, on the opposite side, the countervailing treatment, the means whereby body and mind are kept in health; for it is right to dwell upon good rather than upon evil.

Now the good is always beautiful, and the beautiful never disproportionate; accordingly a living creature that is to possess these qualities must be well-proportioned. Proportions of a trivial kind we readily perceive and compute; but the most important and decisive escape our reckoning. For health or sickness, goodness or badness, the proportion or disproportion between soul and body themselves is more important than any other; yet we pay no heed to this and do not

---

[36] It was a universal doctrine that lethargy was due to phlegm. Wellmann, op. cit., 80¹.

[37] The two causes are a defective constitution inherited from parents and bad upbringing, as is implied by the next sentence.

[38] *Laws* 775d: A man must be careful all through his life, and especially during the time when he is begetting, to commit no act involving either bodily ailment or violence and injustice; for these he will inevitably stamp on the souls and bodies of his offspring.

observe that when a great and powerful soul has for its vehicle a frame too small and feeble, or again when the two are ill-matched in the contrary way, the creature as a whole is not beautiful, since it is deficient in the most important proportions: while the opposite condition is to him who can discern it the fairest and loveliest object of contemplation.[39] Just as a body that is out of proportion because the legs or some other members are too big, is not only ugly, but in the working of one part with another brings countless troubles upon itself with much fatigue and frequent falls due to awkward convulsive movement, so is it, we must suppose, with the composite creature we call an animal. When the soul in it is too strong for the body and of ardent temperament, she dislocates the whole frame and fills it with ailments from within; she wastes it away, when she throws herself into study and research; in teaching and controversy, public or private, she inflames and racks its fabric through the rivalries and contentions that arise, and bringing on rheums deludes most so-called physicians into laying the blame on the unoffending part.[40] On the other hand, when a large body, too big for the soul, is conjoined with a small and feeble mind, whereas the appetites natural to man are of two kinds—desire of food for the body and desire of wisdom for the divinest part in us—the motions of the stronger part prevail and, by augmenting their own power while they make the powers of the soul dull and slow to learn and forgetful, they produce in her the worst of maladies, stupidity.

Now against both these dangers there is one safeguard: not to exercise the soul without the body, nor yet the body with-

---

[39] Language and thought echo the passage describing the love of a beautiful person as the climax of musical education at *Rep.* 402d: "when noble dispositions in the soul are combined in harmony with congruent features of outward form, this is the fairest object of contemplation for one who has eyes to see it . . . and the fairest is also the loveliest."

[40] Note that the soul has its characteristic form of intemperance, which deranges the body, no less than the intemperance of the body, considered in the last section, disorders the soul.

out the soul, in order that both may hold their own and prove
c equally balanced and sound. So the mathematician or one who is intensely occupied with any other intellectual discipline must give his body its due meed of exercise by taking part in athletic training; while he who is industrious in molding his body must compensate his soul with her proper exercise in the cultivation of the mind and all higher education; so one may deserve to be called in the true sense a man of noble breeding. The several parts also should be cared for on the same principle, in imitation of the universal frame. For as
d our body is heated and cooled within by the things that enter it, and again is dried and moistened by what is outside, and suffers affections consequent upon disturbances of both these kinds, if a man surrenders his body to these motions in a state of rest, it is overpowered and ruined. But if he will imitate what we have called the foster-mother and nurse of the universe and never, if possible, allow the body to rest in torpor; if he will keep it in motion and, by perpetually giving it a shake, constantly hold in check the internal and external
e motions in a natural balance; if by thus shaking it in moderation, he will bring into orderly arrangement, one with another, such as we described in speaking of the universe, those affections and particles that wander according to their affinities about the body; then he will not be leaving foe ranged by foe to engender warfare and disease in his body, but will have friend ranged by the side of friend for the production of health.

89 Of motions, again, the best is that motion which is produced in oneself by oneself, since it is most akin to the movement of thought and of the universe; motion produced by another is inferior; and worst of all is that whereby, while the body lies inert, its several parts are moved by foreign agents. Accordingly, of all modes of purifying or bracing the body, the best is gymnastic exercise; next best the swaying motion of a boat or carriage which causes no fatigue; while a
b third kind, though sometimes useful in extreme necessity, should in no other case be employed by a man of sense; I

mean medical purgation by drugs. Disorders should not be irritated by drugs, save where there is grave danger. For in general any disease has a settled constitution somewhat like that of living creatures. The composition of the living creature is so ordered as to have a regular period of life for the species in general; and also each individual by itself is born with its allotted span, apart from inevitable accidents, since the triangles in every creature are from the outset put together with the power to hold out for a certain time, beyond which life cannot be prolonged.[41] It is the same with the constitution of diseases: if this be deranged by drugs to the disregard of their destined period, it often results that slight maladies become grave or their number is increased. Hence, so far as leisure permits, one should manage and control all complaints by regimen, instead of irritating a stubborn mischief by drugs.

## Care of the soul (89d-90d)

Let this suffice for the treatment of the living creature as a whole and of its bodily part, and the way in which a man may best lead a rational life, both governing and being governed by himself. Still more should precedence be given to the training of the part that is destined to govern, so that it may be as perfectly equipped as possible for its work of governance. To treat of this matter in detail would in itself be a sufficient task; but, as a side issue, it may not be out of place to determine the matter in conformity with what has gone before, with these observations. As we have said more than once, there dwell in us three distinct forms of soul, each having its own motions. Accordingly, we may say now as briefly as possible that whichever of these lives in idleness and inactivity with respect to its proper motions must needs become the weakest, while any that is in constant exercise will be strongest; hence we must take care that their motions be kept in due proportion one to another.

[41] Cf. the account of natural death, 81e.

As concerning the most sovereign form of soul in us we must conceive that heaven has given it to each man as a guiding genius—that part which we say dwells in the summit of our body and lifts us from earth toward our celestial affinity, like a plant whose roots are not in earth, but in the heavens. And this is most true, for it is to the heavens, whence the soul first came to birth, that the divine part attaches the head or root of us and keeps the whole body upright. Now if a man is engrossed in appetites and ambitions and spends all his pains upon these, all his thoughts must needs be mortal and, so far as that is possible, he cannot fall short of becoming mortal altogether, since he has nourished the growth of his mortality. But if his heart has been set on the love of learning and true wisdom and he has exercised that part of himself above all, he is surely bound to have thoughts immortal and divine, if he shall lay hold upon truth, nor can he fail to possess immortality in the fullest measure that human nature admits; and because he is always devoutly cherishing the divine part and maintaining the guardian genius that dwells with him in good estate, he must needs be happy above all. Now there is but one way of caring for anything, namely, to give it the nourishment and motions proper to it. The motions akin to the divine part in us are the thoughts and revolutions of the universe; these, therefore, every man should follow, and correcting those circuits in the head that were deranged at birth, by learning to know the harmonies and revolutions of the world, he should bring the intelligent part, according to its pristine nature, into the likeness of that which intelligence discerns, and thereby win the fulfillment of the best life set by the gods before mankind both for this present time and for the time to come.

### *The differentiation of the sexes. The lower animals*
### (90e-92c)

And now, it would seem, we have fairly accomplished the task laid upon us at the outset: to tell the story of the universe so far as to the generation of man: For the manner in which the other living creatures have come into being, brief mention shall be enough, where there is no need to speak at length; so shall we, in our own judgment, rather preserve due measure in our account of them.

Let this matter, then, be set forth as follows. Of those who were born as men, all that were cowardly and spent their life in wrongdoing were, according to the probable account, transformed at the second birth into women: for this reason it was 91 at that time that the gods constructed the desire of sexual intercourse, fashioning one creature instinct with life in us, and another in women. The two were made by them in this way. From the conduit of our drink, where it receives liquid that has passed through the lungs by the kidneys into the bladder and ejects it with the air that presses upon it, they pierced an opening communicating with the compact [42] marrow which runs from the head down the neck and along the spine and has, indeed, in our earlier discourse been called "seed." This marrow, being instinct with life and finding an b outlet, implanted in the part where this outlet was a lively appetite for egress and so brought it to completion as an Eros of begetting. Hence it is that in men the privy member is disobedient and self-willed, like a creature that will not listen to reason, and because of frenzied appetite bent upon carrying all before it. In women again, for the same reason, what is called the matrix or womb, a living creature within them with c a desire for childbearing, if it be left long unfruitful beyond the due season, is vexed and aggrieved, and wandering throughout the body and blocking the channels of the breath, by forbidding respiration brings the sufferer to extreme distress and causes all manner of disorders; until at last the Eros of the one and the Desire of the other bring the pair together, pluck as it were the fruit from the tree [43] and sow the plow- d

---

[42] συμπεπηγότα, forming one connected column, as contrasted with the marrow isolated in other bones.

[43] Cf. 86c, where excess of seed was compared to overabundance of fruit on a tree. The condition is relieved by the plucking of the fruit. The

land of the womb with living creatures still unformed and too small to be seen, and again differentiating their parts nourish them till they grow large within, and thereafter by bringing them to the light of day accomplish the birth of the living creature. Such is the origin of women and of all that is female.

*The lower animals*

Birds were made by transformation: growing feathers instead of hair, they came from harmless but light-witted men, who studied the heavens but imagined in their simplicity that the surest evidence in these matters comes through the eye.

Land animals came from men who had no use for philosophy and paid no heed to the heavens because they had lost the use of the circuits in the head and followed the guidance of those parts of the soul that are in the breast. By reason of these practices they let their forelimbs and heads be drawn down to earth by natural affinity and there supported, and their heads were lengthened out and took any sort of shape into which their circles were crushed together through inactivity. On this account their kind was born with four feet or with many, heaven giving to the more witless the greater number of points of support, that they might be all the more drawn earthward. The most senseless, whose whole bodies were stretched at length upon the earth, since they had no further need of feet, the gods made footless, crawling over the ground.

The fourth sort, that live in water, came from the most foolish and stupid of all. The gods who remolded their form thought these unworthy any more to breathe the pure air, because their souls were polluted with every sort of transgression; and in place of breathing the fine and clean air, they thrust them down to inhale the muddy water of the depths.

---

marrow is, as it were, an inverted tree, with the brain for its root (90a) and the spinal column for its trunk. Democritus (Diels-Kranz, *Vors.*5 68b, 5, p. 137, 13) spoke of plants and trees having their head rooted in earth.

Hence came fishes and shellfish and all that lives in the water: in penalty for the last extreme of folly they are assigned the last and lowest habitation. These are the principles on which, now as then, all living creatures change one into another, shifting their place with the loss or gain of understanding or of folly.

## CONCLUSION (92c)

Here at last let us say that our discourse concerning the universe has come to its end. For having received in full its complement of living creatures, mortal and immortal, this world has thus become a visible living creature embracing all that are visible and an image of the intelligible, a perceptible god, supreme in greatness and excellence, in beauty and perfection, this Heaven single in its kind and one.